FOUR CRITICS

Croce, Valéry,
Lukács, and Ingarden

FOUR CRITICS

Croce, Valéry, Lukács, and Ingarden

By RENÉ WELLEK

UNIVERSITY OF WASHINGTON PRESS

Seattle and London

This book has been published with the assistance of a grant from
the Walker-Ames Fund of the University of Washington.

Library of Congress Cataloging in Publication Data
Wellek, René.
  Four critics.
  Based on four lectures at the University of
Washington, Oct. 11, 18, 24, and Nov. 1, 1979.
  Includes bibliographical references and index.
  1. Criticism—History—20th century—Ad-
dresses, essays, lectures. 2. Croce, Benedetto,
1866–1952—Addresses, essays, lectures. 3.
Valéry, Paul, 1871–1945—Addresses, essays, lec-
tures. 4. Lukács, György, 1885–1971—Ad-
dresses, essays, lectures. 5. Ingarden, Roman,
1893–1970—Addresses, essays, lectures. I. Title.
PN94.W44   801.95′0904   80-54429
ISBN 0-295-95800-6   AACR2

Contents

Preface

This book is based on four lectures given during my tenure as the Walker-Ames Professor at the University of Washington on October 11, 18, 24, and November 1, 1979. They were to provide a conspectus of twentieth-century continental criticism, not, of course, as anything like an encyclopedic survey but as presenting vantage-points from which we can view the scene with some confidence of looking into all the four corners of the landscape. As a surveyor is not obliged to measure every foot of ground he triangulates, so the expounder of critical doctrines has to choose the prominent figures who hold sharply contrasting doctrines in order to suggest that the rest of most possible positions are located somewhere in between. I have chosen these four critics because they seem to fulfill this requirement almost ideally.

Benedetto Croce, the Italian aesthetician, developed a critical theory in which the distinction between author, work, and reader are obliterated in a single act of intuition-expression. Paul Valéry, the French poet, in contrast, keeps the three stages of the aesthetic transaction completely separate. There is the creative activity of man, there is the work which should be as pure and perfect and impersonal as possible, and there is the reader who can do with the work whatever he pleases, read or misread it. In Croce, poetry is a single creative act of the mind: what is external is not any more a work of art. At most the production of a work is due to the desire of the artist to perpetuate and communicate to others his inner creative act. In Valéry, writing is making, even manufacturing. The baker is not similar to the bread he makes, the man who eats the bread needs no knowledge of the baker. The monistic spiritualism of Croce stands against Valéry's Cartesianism.

Similarly, our second pair, the Hungarian Marxist Georg Lukács and the Polish philosopher Roman Ingarden, present a striking contrast. Lukács conceives of literature as an index and mirror of society and reality, sees it as deeply involved and even determined by historical process and still wants it to influence the course of history. Ingarden, on the other hand, as a follower of Edmund Husserl, the founder of phenomenology, focuses all his attention on the work itself, which exists as a construct with a peculiarly independent mode of being. He contemplates it intently, analyzes it into layers, and studies its effects on the reader without attention to its antecedents in the author or presumed causes in society or history.

No doubt, another group of four critics could have been chosen. But I have published papers on Russian formalism and on the Czech group around the Prague Linguistic Circle who called themselves structuralists as early as 1934. I have also written on Walter Benjamin, the Marxist who remained, in spite of his political commitment, a Jewish mystic; on Albert Thibaudet, the French Bergsonian; and on Friedrich Gundolf and Max Kommerell, the followers, faithful and unfaithful, of Stefan George, the German poet who set himself up as a prophet of an austere creed. I have published elaborate papers on the three great Romance scholars: Ernst Robert Curtius, Leo Spitzer, and Erich Auerbach. No lecturer likes to say things he has said elsewhere and possibly better in print. Still, eventually I hope to collect and synthesize all these intellectual portraits in the sixth volume of my *History of Modern Criticism*.

For the convenience of the reader, the notes include references to published translations when these exist, although frequently I have provided my own translations rather than quoting those already published.

May 1981   René Wellek

FOUR CRITICS

Croce, Valéry,
Lukács, and Ingarden

Benedetto Croce
(1866–1952)

Benedetto Croce's aesthetics is by far the most influential of the twentieth century, not only in Italy, where it has monopolized the field, but also in most other countries of the West: in England, Robin G. Collingwood and Edgar F. Carritt can be described as Croceans; in the United States, Joel E. Spingarn was a propounder of a simplified Croceanism; and John Crowe Ransom, the father of the New Criticism, refers to Croce at crucial points. In Germany the whole group of Romance scholars, Karl Vossler, Leo Spitzer, Erich Auerbach, can be called Crocean; his influence is also visible in Spain and Latin America. It seems, however, almost nonexistent in France and Russia. Croce's dominant position in Italy is not only, of course, due to his aesthetics: it is the combined effect of all the activities of a man who excelled in almost every branch of learning. Croce devised a whole system of philosophy in which logic, economics, and ethics have their coordinate place with aesthetics. But beyond this systematic philosophizing Croce has, even more importantly, been concerned with the theory and practice of historiography and with politics, in which he took an active part as a symbol of anti-Fascism, as the last great Liberal. Most significantly for us, Croce was an eminent practical critic of current literature and the great classics and an immensely erudite literary scholar. I believe that in the whole history of criticism, only Sainte-Beuve and Wilhelm Dilthey can match him, and then I am not sure whether Croce does not surpass them. But outside of Italy, Croce's impact was largely confined to the aesthetics; many of his other writings are not translated, though in English one can get a sampling of his literary criticism. His *Goethe* (1919), his *Dante* (1921), the volume on *Ariosto, Shakespeare, Corneille* (1920), and the book of essays on *Poesia e non Poesia* (1923), called *European Literature in the Nineteenth Century*, are available in English; but not *La Poesia* (1936) or the mass of smaller writings, except for a wide-ranging anthology, *Philosophy, Poetry, History*.[1]

Croce's aesthetics, though widely quoted and referred to, and basically quite simple in its radicalism, upholds a position which is easy to misunderstand. A full study would have to distinguish between the four or five phases of Croce's evolution: the early preliminary stage in which the little book *La Critica Letteraria* (1894) interests us most; the period of *Estetica* (1902); the new version, *Breviario di Estetica*, written in 1912 for the opening of the Rice Institute at Houston, Texas; *Aesthetica in Nuce* (1928), a third brief version, first in the 14th edition of the *Encyclopedia Britannica*; and finally *La Poesia* (1936).

The main thesis known, I suppose, to everybody, is that art is intuition. One must, in order to understand Croce's term, forget about mystical intuition (that is always dismissed by Croce, who is resolutely secular). Intuition is the same as "representation," *Anschauung*. It is not "sensation," which in Croce's terminology is mere passive formless matter; it is not "perception," which is the apprehension of something real. Intuition thus is a far wider category than what we would ordinarily call "art," and Croce's aesthetics, while in practice concerned mainly with the realm of art, assumes a complete continuity between ordinary "representations," also in memory, e.g., of *this* river, *this* lake, *this* brook, *this* rain, *this* glass of water (called intuitions), and language and art. Croce expressly denies that one can draw a line between intuitions that are called "art" and those that are vulgarly called "not art." But we have not understood Croce's definition if we do not immediately add his identification of intuition with expression. Expression, of course, in Croce, does not necessarily mean verbal expression: it might be expression by line, color, or sound. Verbal expression again need not be speaking aloud nor, of course, writing: an intuition may be expressed (but even this dualism is false, since intuition *is* expression) without any outward action. Thus, all language is part of aesthetics, is expression, is creation. Croce's intuition-expression is the activity of the human mind which *precedes*, in his philosophical scheme, that of conceptual knowledge. Still, intuition-expression is knowledge, theoretical (not practical) activity, but knowledge of things in their concreteness and individuality, not conceptual knowledge.

Once we have understood in what sense Croce uses intuition, we shall not be surprised at the consequences he draws. Art (that is intuition-expression) he will argue, is, first, not a physical fact: neither a stone nor a canvas nor a piece of paper.

Secondly, art is not pleasure. The feeling of pleasure and pain belongs to the realm of the practical. Pleasure does not distinguish the aesthetic fact from other facts: pleasure may be sexual, organic (visceral), etc.; in short, it may accompany all activities of man but it does not single out the world of art. It is impossible to discover any special aesthetic pleasure. To define art as pleasure is like defining fish by the water in which they swim.

Thirdly, art is not morality, as morality is a practical act, which follows after intuition and knowledge. Still it is a gross misunderstanding to think of Croce as an aesthete who denies the moral and social responsibility of the artist. He would say that "the artist will always be morally blameless and philosophically irreproachable, even though his art may have for subject matter a low morality and philosophy: insofar as he is an artist, he does not act and not reason, but ~~paints~~, sings; in short, expresses himself." [2] E~~x~~ternalization, reproduction, and diffusion of th~~e~~ ~~intui~~tion is a practical act and can be regulated by socie~~ty~~ allow censorship and even the burning of perniciou~~s~~ Nobody is more violent than Croce in his condemnation of aestheticism and decadentism as it was understood late in the nineteenth century: it is to him the attempt to make aesthetics the standard of morality. In Italy, D'Annunzio and Marinetti prefigure Fascism.

Fourthly, art is neither science nor philosophy. Croce over and over again insists that art is not conceptual knowledge, that it does not present ideas or universals, that "he who begins to think scientifically has already ceased to contemplate aesthetically." [3] Conceptual knowledge is always knowledge of the real, aiming at distinguishing between the real and the unreal, while intuition means precisely "indistinction of reality and unreality, the *image* with its value as mere image, the pure ideality of the image." [4] Croce considers thus intellectualistic all theories that make art "symbolic of a reality," all theories that put the aim of art into the typical or generic, and all theories that make art a version of religion or myth (to Croce rudimentary forms of philosophy).

If we have understood this central identification of art with intuition and expression, we shall be better prepared for the shock of some of the conclusions Croce draws from his position: as intuition is a generally human faculty, there is no special artistic genius. Instead of "the poet is born," we should say, "Man is born a poet." There is, of course, no distinction between content and form. Content to Croce would be, at most, brute matter preceding the act of intuition. But we can know nothing about it. Croce, at times, can say that "the aesthetic fact is form and nothing but form" and that the aesthetic of intuition could be called the "Aesthetic of form." Thus Croce is often simply considered a formalist. But this is quite misleading if we mean by formalism anything like what he would condemn as abstract academic formalism. Actually Croce admits that what he calls form could just as well be called content. "It is merely a question of terminological convenience, whether we should describe art as content or as form, provided it be always understood that the content is formed and the form filled, that feeling is figured feeling and the figure a figure that is felt." [5] In practice, Croce constantly minimizes what are usually called the "formal elements of art" and is interested in intuition, which to him is form but which could also be described as feeling, or pervasive content. If one reads Croce's practical criticism, it is obvious that he has very little interest in form in the usual sense but always tries to define the leading sentiment of an author. Because in Croce there is only this one act of intuition, the one distinction between art and non-art, the description of the differences between works of art and authors is reduced to elements that many would call "content"—not, of course, to the raw material outside of art, to the mere theme or plot, but to the feelings, attitudes, and preoccupations embodied in the work of art.

If there is no distinction between content and form, each work of art is indivisible, forms a unity, an organic whole, that cannot be divided, except for purely practical purposes. Hence, a work of art cannot be translated. There are no rhetorical categories, no such distinctions as those between romanticism and classicism, no need of a word such as *style*, which at most is a synonym for expression. "In the aesthetic fact there are none but proper words: the same intuition can be expressed in one way only." [6] If every work of art is simply successful expression, Croce can resolutely expel from aesthetics (or, at least *his* aesthetics) all categories such as the tragic, the sublime, the comic, and the humorous. They are simply handed over to psychology; they are only empirical, unconnected, descriptive terms derived from an aesthetics of sympathy irrelevant, or rather extra-aesthetic, in Croce's scheme.

The theory so far hangs together and is quite coherent if we once understand what it is about: this intuition-expression. One would think that in practice it would lead to critical paralysis, since we are deprived of the majority of terms and concepts with which criticism worked and works. Indeed, Croce's theory of criticism is a highly untheoretical one: it merely says that the critic must reproduce the work of art in himself. Creator, work, and auditor or reader are identified more closely than in any other system. If criticism is identification with the creator, taste and genius must be identical. Croce logically rejects any critical absolutism in the sense of judging according to some canon or models that would be intellectual concepts. But he also rejects critical relativism, which would deny the possibility of this identification. In this scheme which has to recognize the frequent failure of this meeting of minds, great importance is assigned to the role of criticism as historical interpretation, as a restoration of the conditions that make the identification of the reader with the author possible. But erudition is considered only as auxiliary work toward comprehension. Criticism, while using all these tools, simply calls into existence a certain internal activity, aesthetic reproduction, which is fundamentally the same as the intuition of the artist.

In the idealistic theory of knowledge assumed by Croce, all these three sides—the author's creative intuition, his expression, and the reader's comprehension—are identical activities. The work of art as a physical fact is considered by Croce merely the result of a volitional act of externalization. "When we have fixed an intuition, we have still to decide whether or no we should communicate it to others, and to whom, and when, and how; all which deliberations come equally under the utilitarian and ethical criterion." This externalization is understood as a "taking measure by the artist against losing the result of his spiritual labor, and in favor of rendering possible or easy, for himself and for others, the reproduction of his images." Hence he engages in practical acts that assist the work of reproduction. These practical acts are guided by knowledge, and for this reason are called technical. Technique is thus something external, with the result in Croce's system that we must and can dismiss all the classifications of the arts. Croce is very violent about this: "Any attempt at an aesthetic classification of the arts is absurd. . . . All the books dealing with classification and systems of the arts could be burned without any loss whatever." [7]

If there is no classification of the arts (only practical knowledge useful for the artist about, say, the ways of casting in bronze, or the technique of mixing colors, or the conventions of harmony), we need hardly say that Croce completely rejects the concept of literary kinds. The kinds have, at the most, a purely classificatory function such as, for instance, the Dewey decimal system in a library. "Who can deny the necessity and utility of such arrangements? But what should be said if some one began seriously to seek out the literary laws . . . of shelf A or shelf B, that is to say, of these altogether arbitrary groupings whose sole object was their practical utility." Artists have always disregarded these so-called laws of the kinds. "Every true work of art has violated some established kind and upset the ideas of the critics." The traditional three kinds—lyric, epic, drama—are not really distinguishable. In every lyric, there is epic and drama; in every drama, lyric and epic. No lyric is purely subjective: it is addressed to others; every epic and drama expresses the author. But Croce need not argue the detail of genre theories. He can say simply: "No intermediate element interposes itself philosophically between the universal and the particular, no series of kinds or species, or *generalia*." [8]

This view of the externalization of intuition as a different practical activity, with its corollary, which denies the aesthetic relevance of technique and even of the distinctions of the arts and the genres, has aroused most opposition to Croce's theories. But the whole position can be and is usually misunderstood if we think that Croce simply argues in favor of an internal vision of the artist that is unique and undifferentiated and *then* is translated in a second practical, inferior act into a painting, a poem, or a piece of sculpture or music. Croce sometimes speaks in a manner open to such misinterpretation. But we always must remember that intuition with Croce is not inner vision but is also expression. He argues that "when the intuition has been distinguished from the expression, and the one has been made different from the other, no ingenuity in inventing middle terms can reunite them."[9] But he insists on the difference between expression and technique.

I am not convinced by Croce's total monistic idealism and am particularly dissatisfied by his handling of the problem of externalization and communication. I believe that there is a clear distinction between poetry, which can be composed in the mind, and the plastic arts, which need an external medium to define and elaborate the intuition. Poetry in the mind is a bird in the hand; painting and architecture in the mind is a bird in the bush. Still, one should recognize that the system is not open to ordinary empirical objections and that it can be refuted only by rejecting its basic epistemology. "What is called *external* is no longer a work of art," is irrefutable in Croce's terms.[10]

It is surprising that with this series of identifications—intuition and expression, vision and the external work of art—Croce has been able to handle concretely so many authors and works. Actually, in the later formulations of his theories, Croce introduced some modifications of his central concept of intuition-expression, which, in the early *Aesthetic*, is purely of the individual. Later, Croce emphasizes the universalizing character of art for which he invents the term *cosmicità*. While he still insists on the difference between art and concept, intuition and abstraction, he can say that art "links the particular to the universal." This universality is a synonym of the "total and indivisible humanity of its vision," though it is found only in the particular work of art.[11] Here Croce comes near the concept of the "concrete universal" (though he always criticized Hegel for false intellectualism), and even of the symbol. Croce, however, dismisses "symbol" as an unnecessary concept, false if it means symbol of something and superfluous if it means the unity of the particular and the general which is the nature of expression-intuition. Croce is no nominalist if one defines nominalism as saying that "only words are universals." Words in poetry are with him particulars if they are intuition-expressions and not concepts. There are two kinds of language: original poetic and conceptual-communicative.

Croce, in his later versions of his aesthetics, emphasizes that intuition-expression must not be misunderstood as a recommendation of emotionalism and spontaneity as such, as the "overflow of feelings," as romanticism in the vulgar sense. But his practice and vocabulary often leaves itself open to misunderstanding. He seems proud of having introduced the term *liricità* and of arguing that all poetry is lyrical. But neither the etymology of the word nor its associations, at least in English or German, prepare us for the identification of lyricism with poetry itself. For Croce poetry is "passion" but not violent confused passion and is not restricted to the romantic passions of love or despair. Passions can be, he says, "expressive of security of thought, calm firmness of will, moderated energy, virtue, faith and the like." [12] Art is always theoretical expression of sentiment, sentiment transformed into an image. Croce thus can advocate *classicità* which is of course not academic classicism. He always remained opposed to art being too obviously craft, too obviously intellectual or oratorical. Hence his dislike for the baroque and for symbolism as well as allegory (which by definition cannot be poetic).

Also in the theory of criticism, Croce modified his early position which put the aim of criticism into an identification with the author. He had gone so far as to say, "If I penetrate to the innermost sense of a canto of Dante's, I am Dante." [13] But later Croce, more wisely, saw that criticism is rather a translation from the realm of feeling into the realm of thought. He found that critics should be reminded of the prohibition he had seen posted in some German concert halls, "Das Mitsingen ist verboten." [14] The objection that criticism moves into a sphere completely remote from art is countered by Croce's argument that thought is the beginning of a new sentiment and act, that better understanding means deeper enjoyment.

But this change to a more theoretical ideal of criticism is not complete. Croce still insists that the aim of criticism is the characterization of the individual author, the essay, and monograph, and he denies the possibility of an internal history of art. Art is a historical fact in Croce, as in Croce everything which occurs in the mind is history. But the work of art is a monument and not a document and is thus immediately accessible to the mind. Thus any poet should be judged in terms of poetry here and now and everywhere. He cannot be judged as a link in a chain, as part of a history of art, as in Croce there is no such history, beyond the historical facts of individual works and beyond the social setting.

Thus Croce was no friend of the usual *comparatisme*, the studies of themes and motifs, sources and influences, for their own sake. In reviewing the prospectus of Woodberry, Fletcher, and Spingarn's ill-fated *Journal of Comparative Literature*, in 1903, Croce asked pointedly: What is comparative literature? If it means the comparative method, then it obviously goes far beyond literature and is constantly used in the study of even a single author. If it means the tracing of literary themes and influences, it is useful but leaves us with a feeling of emptiness. "These are merely erudite investigations, which in themselves do not make us understand a literary work and do not make us penetrate into the living core of artistic creation." [15] They refer only to the after-history of a work already formed (its fame, translations, imitations, etc.) or to the materials that may have contributed to its origins. But if we define comparative literature as the study of all antecedents of a work of art, philosophical and literary, then it is identical with all literary history and the word *comparative* is really a pleonasm. There is only a choice between mere literary erudition and a truly historical and interpretative method.

Croce thus attacked the concept of literary history as an evolutionary process. He criticized severely what he called the sociological concept of literary history exemplified for him in all romantic histories of literature which conceive of literature as an expression of a national spirit, and *a fortiori* in all positivistic histories which make literature directly reflect a specific ideology (Georg Brandes) or explain it in terms of race and milieu (Hippolyte Taine). Croce, of course, recognized the immense advance which such historiography, in the hands of the Schlegels or Taines, represented, as compared to the purely erudite accumulations of eighteenth-century learning. But he also saw that it made literature a product of something else, that it confused art with the intellectual and practical forms of the spirit (with philosophy and morality). When he was confronted with the theories and practice of Heinrich Wölfflin, who advocated a history of art that would be a truly internal history of its development, of its devices, techniques, and assumptions, Croce also refused to accept this solution of the problem. It follows from his aesthetic theory that devices and techniques, rhetorical categories and genres, get short shrift. Such history appeared to Croce an arid academic exercise or at most a history of fashions and customs, a history of civilization that has nothing essential to say to a man interested in the central problem of criticism—the intuition-expression of the poet.

In his proposal for a "reform of the history of literature and art," [16] he argued that the only proper literary history is the *caratteristica* (critical characterization) of a single artist, of both his personality and his work, which form a whole. The unit thus will always been an essay or a monograph.

Croce substantially followed his own advice and instincts and steadily produced a stream of essays, of "characterizations," which focus sharply on the one problem he considered essential. "Criticism," he said in a letter summarizing a conversation I had with him on June 5 in Naples in the year of his death, 1952, "does not require anything else than to know the true sentiment of the poet in the representative form in which he has translated it. Any other demand is extraneous to the

question." If one asks that the series of monographs and critical essays be put into some order, the answer is that "everyone
can put it into any order he pleases." There is no continuity
(except an external one) between Dante, Boccaccio, and Pe-
trarch, or Pulci, Boiardo, and Ariosto. They are all different,
and the critic's task is to grasp, to describe, and thus implicitly
to evaluate their individuality, their uniqueness. Croce has done
this in hundreds of essays which take up practically every figure of Italian literature. He began writing such practical criticism in 1903 when he founded the periodical *La Critica*, which
he filled with his own contributions almost to the end of his
life, though he had some collaborators such as the philosopher
Giovanni Gentile in the early years. At first, he concentrated
on the contemporary or near-contemporary literature of Italy,
severely judging what he considered the decadence, the mis-
taken aestheticism of the late nineteenth century. D'Annunzio,
Fogazzaro, Pascoli and later Pirandello were his main victims,
while Carducci remained his lifelong favorite. Only very late,
after World War II, did Croce modify the severity of his judgments in a more tolerant, even mellow mood. In many essays
he also reexamined the whole of older Italian literature, condemning the baroque age for its "silence of great poetry"[17] and
picking his way through Renaissance and eighteenth-century
literature, anthologizing, singling out poems and passages that
appealed to his taste and fitted in with his view of poetry.

From contemporary Italian literature, his criticism moved
increasingly into the past and into other countries. Croce's
book on Goethe is a most refreshing book of the Goethe literature I know. It is entirely free from the usual German in-
discriminate idolatry of Goethe and even his slightest works,
and yet expresses great admiration, love, and understanding
for what is genuinely great in the man and the poet. Croce
achieves his success by resolutely divorcing the question of the
poet's personality and biography from a judgment of the works
themselves. He is entirely aware of the interest elicited by
Goethe's personality, biography and "wisdom," etc. But he

resolutely declines to fuse and confuse the two things, biography and criticism, and constantly points out the pitfalls of the biographical and psychological methods.

For the actual judgment of Goethe's poetry, Croce's view is also refreshingly new: he again brushes aside the usual intellectualism which looks for profundities and philosophical truth at any cost. Croce, though he does not use this term, is well aware of the "intentional fallacy" and therefore ignores or discounts all of Goethe's professions and intentions. He applies "the good old rule that with poets one must look not for what they wished or asserted that they were doing but what they did do poetically." Croce thus can treat *Faust* as almost an album in which Goethe entered his feelings at different times of his life. He can dismiss the tortuous attempts to find a coherence between the early version in the *Urfaust* or even in the Prologue in Heaven and the final scene of *Faust II*. He can see that in *Faust I* we have to deal with two fairly separate plays, the pact with the Devil and the story of Gretchen, and that *Faust II* is also pieced together from the *Helena* tragedy, long, allegorical, almost operatic pageants and the final scenes which, as Croce shows convincingly, are full of the old Goethe's sly humor and parody and must not be taken too solemnly. Goethe desired, no doubt, to give fictitious unity to his fragments, but Croce rejects this search for unity and defends himself skillfully against the objection that his criticism destroys the organism created by the poet. The opposite is true: "The poet, by a reflective proposition, has erected a mechanism, which encloses and compresses several and diverse living organisms." [18] Croce consistently combats the view that philosophical, conceptual poetry is the highest poetry. The truly profound poetry in *Faust* is in the Easter scene or in the Jail scene of Part I, while the allegories or symbols of *Faust II* are often dead and abstract. Croce appreciates most highly the early Goethe and has little use for what is usually called his "classicism." The early poetry is the most "classical" in Croce's sense because it is most free from intellectualistic and moralistic admixtures.

The same basic thesis is behind the little book on Dante (1921). This book caused an enormous debate and could hardly convince by the radical distinction there drawn between the "theological-political romance," the structure as an abstract scheme, and the poetry which grows around it like luxurious vegetation.

Both the Dante and Goethe books make an effort to elaborate what to Croce must always be the central critical problem: the distinction between poetry and nonpoetry, or between poetry which is "classical," i.e., a successful union of inspiration and discipline, expression and image, and poetry which is mere feeling, mere emotion, poetry which is purely oratorical, directed toward a practical effect, or poetry which is intellectualistic, didactic, instructive. A late book, *La poesia* (1936), works out these distinctions most clearly, sharply discriminating also between poetry and literature—"literature" meaning writing in its civilizing function. The volume of little essays, *Poesia e non poesia* (1923), which in the English translation is called *European Literature in the Nineteenth Century* (1924), is an early application of these criteria and distinctions to figures somewhat haphazardly picked from the nineteenth century. Thus Schiller is put down as a philosophical rhetorician, thus Heinrich von Kleist is described as a poet merely striving by will power to become one, while George Sand is severely judged as propounder of the gospel of romantic love, a case history for a moment of civilization, not a true artist. Sir Walter Scott appears to Croce to be merely a manufacturer of books, a "hero of industry," [19] and an antiquarian who approaches poetry only in rare moments of human kindness; while Maupassant is highly appreciated though shown to be limited to one theme and one feeling. These distinctions are also applied with vigor within the work of an author. Thus Leopardi, in an essay that caused much offense, is disparaged as a thinker and shown to be very limited in the expression of his own feeling—disappointment with life—while he achieved poetry in Croce's sense of serenity only in the idylls.

The method is always one and the same. Croce selects what he considers poetry, brushes aside what is something else, and tries to define a leading sentiment, something like Taine's *faculté maîtresse*, which allows him to characterize by constant qualifications. Two essays out of the three collected in the book *Ariosto, Shakespeare, Corneille* (1920) are particularly striking examples. Ariosto is shown to be inspired by a desire for cosmic harmony which pervades every single sentiment of his work and all his language and meter, a poetic Hegel; Corneille is dominated by one passion, the ideal of free will. Each essay reaches what seems to me a rather meager conclusion by a process of elimination, by surveying the different solutions given by other critics, since Croce believes that the process of criticism is also a historical process, a dialectical argument against and with others. The essay on Shakespeare, though it contains a fine execution of conventional and foolish Shakespeare scholarship, seems to me inferior; Croce does not, I think, see into the tragic depth of Shakespeare or grasp his intense power of language, but he formulates excellently his feeling for life and his strong sense of right and wrong. Croce is falsely judged if we think of his criticism as narrowly aesthetic; it is, rather, strongly ethical, even "psychological," if, of course, we recognize that he distinguishes between an empirical and a poetic personality, and studies only the latter.

The enduring importance of Croce for the student of literature, however, may, paradoxically, rest less on his strictly literary criticism and history than on his aesthetics and his history of aesthetics and in his theory and history of historiography.

Two-thirds of the *Estetica* is a history of aesthetics. His rediscovery of Vico as an aesthetician, hardly appreciated in his significance before Croce, expounded in a special book,[20] his discussions of Alexander Gottlieb Baumgarten (who coined the term *Aesthetic* in 1735) and Friedrich Schleiermacher, and especially his many expositions, defenses, and comments on Francesco De Sanctis, the great historian of Italian literature, are major contributions to any history of critical thought. I feel that Croce is sometimes too much preoccupied with tracing only the one line of thought anticipating his own central conceptions; but his enormous erudition, his analytical power, his skill in marshaling facts and pulling together what seems remote is so great that every article of his is worth meditating and digesting.

His literary criticism, in the strict sense, appears to me thus limited. It is inspired by a clear philosophy and basic pathos; but it seems more seriously limited by a specific taste than his more freely ranging philosophical and aesthetic speculations. It does not stand or fall with our acceptance of his system of aesthetics *in toto*, but is circumscribed by a personal taste which is also that of a particular time. He rejects the baroque and much of what we would admire most in modern poetry since Baudelaire. Mallarmé and Valéry are his pet aversions. Croce himself had a ruling sentiment, was a historical personality in his own sense, unique even in his limitations, as we all are.

Paul Valéry
(1871–1945)

The poetic theory of Paul Valéry can be seen as almost the direct opposite of that of Croce: in Croce we find the most complete identification of the author's creative act with the work of art and the response of the reader, the most emphatic devaluation of what ordinarily is called for in favor of sentiment, the strongest feeling for the historicity of literature. In Valéry we are confronted with a theory that asserts the discontinuity between author, work, and reader, emphasizes a most extreme regard for form and nothing but form divorced from emotion, and takes poetry completely out of history into a realm of the pure and the absolute.[1]

Valéry expounded his poetics in a systematic fashion only once: in the course on poetics he gave at the Collège de France from 1937 to 1945. He published only the introductory lecture, and the meager notes published in *Ygdrassil* by George Le Breton covering eighteen lectures between 25 December, 1937 and 25 February, 1939 add little. The lecture moves in the confines of preliminary philosophical considerations. A study of the mass of notes accumulated by Valéry during his so-called silence (from 1892 to 1917)[2] and a complete transcript of the course hardly changes what we already know from Valéry's considered pronouncements in the published essays, collected mainly in the five volumes of *Variété* (1924–44) and in *Pièces sur l'art* (1931), in the essays in *Poësie* (1928), in "Réflexions sur l'art" (1935), in scattered prefaces, addresses, and in the great number of aphorisms throughout volumes such as *Mélange* (1941) and *Tel Quel* (2 vols., 1941–42). Valéry is not a systematic philosopher or aesthetician: he propounds a number of insights which are sometimes, at least, superficially contradictory; he is, within a very limited range, a practical critic and above all a practicing poet who examines the creative process or speculates about his craft. He implicitly raises fundamental questions without often claiming or attempting to solve them within a consistent framework.

Much of the interest of Valéry's thought lies precisely in its tentativeness, in its suggestiveness, in its extremism which, however, is held only provisionally, often for the sake of a specific argument or as a contradiction to accepted opinions, in order to surprise or shock, to experiment with a thought, to see where it will lead.

Valéry, like many other theorists, sharply distinguishes between the author, the work, and the reader, but he goes further than any other writer I know in doubting the continuity and even the desirability of continuity among the three. He complains that in most aesthetics one finds "a confusion of considerations some of which make sense only for the author, others are valid only for the work, and yet others only for the person who experiences the work. Any proposition which brings together these three entities is illusory." He would assert more positively that "producer and consumer are two essentially separate systems,"[3] and most boldly that the "art, as value, depends essentially on this nonidentification (of producer and consumer), this need for an intermediary between producer and consumer."[4] Valéry summarizes:

In short, a work of art is an object, a human product [*fabrication*], made with a view to affecting certain individuals in a cer-

tain way. The phenomenon Art can be represented by two perfectly distinct transformations (It is the same relation as that in
economics between production and consumption). What is extremely important to note is that the two transformations—the
one which goes from the author to the *manufactured object* and
the one which expresses the fact that the object or the work mod-
ifies the consumer—are entirely independent. It follows that
one should always consider them separately.[5]

Thus, art is *not* communication, certainly not direct communication between authors and readers. "If what has hap-
pened in the one person were communicated directly to the
other, all art would collapse, all the effects of art would disappear."[6] Art would become rhetoric, persuasion. Thus, "the
mutual independence of the producer and the consumer, their
ignorance of each other's thoughts and needs is almost essential to the effect of a work."[7] But it is hard to see how such a
theory can be upheld in its extreme formulation: if the gulf
between creator, work, and reader were unbridgeable, there
would be no works and the works (if existent) would be completely incomprehensible. But although Valéry tries out the
theory without quite seeing its consequences, he is right when
he emphasizes the difficulties of these relationships: Has the
work anything to do with the author? Has the reader's interpretation of a work anything to do with its supposed "real"
meaning? He answers "very little," but to my mind he can
hardly answer "nothing at all."

If we isolate the three factors and begin with the author, we
can see that Valéry has the courage of his conviction and is
really not so much or not primarily interested in the product,
the work of art, as in the process of production, the creative
process independent of its result. As a matter of fact, if one
wanted to explain the psychological or genetic origin of Valéry's theory, one would probably find that it started with his
interest in the creative process and was motivated by it. Valéry
is interested in this activity in itself and has thus created the
somewhat monstrous self-caricature, Monsieur Teste: he has

written elaborately about Leonardo da Vinci, the universal man. When, in a formal, rather empty anniversary speech, he praised Goethe in the terms he had used for Leonardo, he implicitly praised himself or rather the ideal he had set up for himself. Goethe is the potential creator, who has the genius of transformation, of metamorphosis; he is Orpheus, Proteus.[8] Goethe's speculations on metamorphosis and evolution attract Valéry more than his poetry. He admires the combination of scientist and poet. Valéry's thought moves so much on this very general level of human creativeness that he can assimilate artistic creativeness to scientific creativeness by some general term such as *speculation*. The essay on Edgar Allan Poe's *Eureka* is inspired by such an identification (or by the hope for such an identification) of science and poetry through the common element of imagination, though Valéry avoids the term.[9]

If one is interested in the creative process as such, one will disparage the work of art. This is what Valéry does, both in words and in deeds. During his many years of silence, he obviously felt that he was elaborating his ideas and his personality, and that expression and especially publication were purely secondary to this inner activity. "The Great Work for me is knowing work as such—knowing the most general transformation, of which the works are only local applications, particular problems." Thus the work of art is conceived as existing only in the act. "Poetry is essentially *in actu*."[10]

> A work of mind exists only in action. Outside of that act, nothing is left but an object which has no particular relation to the mind. Transport a statue which you admire to a country sufficiently different from ours and it turns into a meaningless stone, a Parthenon into nothing more than a small marble quarry. And when a piece of poetry is used as a collection of grammatical difficulties or examples, it ceases immediately to be a work of the mind, since the use that is made of it is utterly alien to the conditions under which it came into being, while, at the same time, it is denied the consumption value that gives it meaning.[11]

Implicitly, of course, the discontinuity is here deplored or considered as a condition to be overcome under ideal circumstances, but the emphasis remains on the act of composing, not on its result. Thus Valéry could tell an interviewer that a work of art is never finished, that we deliver it to the public only under the pressure of external circumstances.[12] We can only abandon it. Valéry always assumes that there is first a thought and then its artistic dress, or rather shape or form. Too ready communication of the thought would prejudice the artistic process.

It is not surprising that Valéry has given us several minute introspective accounts of the composition of his poems and that he excels in this analysis. But whatever the specific interest of these "marvels of introspection," as T. S. Eliot calls them, Valéry arrives, of necessity, at very little for theory, since his introspection leads to the conclusion that there is no direct relationship between a specific state of mind of the author and the work itself. Indeed, there might be a very considerable distance between the original idea, the germ of the work, and the finished product. The organic analogy of begetting, growing, and being born is rejected: there is no continuity between the act of conception and the work produced. The germ of a work of art can be anything: "Sometimes a certain subject, sometimes a group of words, sometimes a simple rhythm, sometimes (even) a prosodic scheme. . . . It is important to remember that one germ may be as good as another. . . . An empty sheet of paper; an idle moment; a slip of the tongue; a misreading; a pen that is pleasant to hold." Anything might suggest the germ of the poem. The poetic state is "perfectly irregular, inconstant, involuntary, fragile . . . we lose it, as we obtain it, *by accident*." One could call this a theory of inspiration, but Valéry is very reluctant to admit inspiration. "I believed and still believe that it is ignoble to write from enthusiasm alone. Enthusiasm is not a state of mind for a writer." Inspiration is no guarantee of the value of the product. "The spirit blows where it listeth: one sees it blow on fools."[13]

If poetry or art in general is not inspiration, it is obviously not dream. In an age in which *surréalisme*, Freudianism, and symbolism asserted the kinship of poetry and dream, Valéry repudiates it emphatically, though he recognizes that "the poetic universe bears strong analogies to the universe of dreams," and that as an historical fact, this confusion between poetry and dream has been understandable since the time of romanticism. But, "the true condition of a true poet is as distinct as possible from the state of dreaming. In the former I can see nothing but voluntary efforts, suppleness of thought, a submission of the mind to exquisite constraints, and the perpetual triumph of sacrifice. . . . Whoever speaks of exactness of style invokes the opposite of dream." [14]

Though Valéry recognizes some initial irrational suggestion such as two rhythms insisting on being heard, as he describes it in "Mémoires d'un poème," [15] all the practical emphasis falls on the share of rational speculation after the moment of conception, on the poetic calculus, on the poet's exercise of choice among possibilities, his clairvoyant, highly conscious pursuit of a sport or game. Valéry loves to think of the art of poetry as "a sport of people insensitive to the conventional values of common language." He says, in slightly different terms, that a poem is "a game, but a solemn, regulated, significant game" or "a kind of calculus" or an algebra. Thus "every true poet is necessarily a critic of the first order," but, of course, this criticism by no means makes the poet a philosopher. Valéry, surprisingly enough in view of his intellectualism, sharply divorces poetry from philosophy, not as an act, but in its result. "Every true poet," he admits, "is much more capable than is generally known of right reasoning and abstract thinking." Still, philosophical poetry is impossible, is not even a possible idea. Valéry disparages poet-philosophers such as Alfred de Vigny. He can say that "to philosophize in verse, was and still is the same as if one wanted to play chess by the rules of the game of checkers." [16]

What Valéry demands of poetry is always something pure,

something *sui generis*, and thus poetry cannot be continuous with the personality of the author; it is and must be impersonal to be perfect. "Perfection eliminates the person of the author," or even more strongly: "I don't see what something that keeps reminding me of the man behind it has to do with art. . . . The writer's duty, his proper function, is to fade out of the picture, to obliterate himself, his face, his personal concerns, his love affairs. . . . What makes a work is not the man who signs it. What makes a work has no name." What Valéry admires in poetry is the effort of men such as Victor Hugo and Stéphane Mallarmé (one is surprised at this pairing) "to form non-human ways of discourse, absolute discourse, in a sense—discourse which suggests a certain being independent of any person—a divinity of language." [17] The continuity between author and work is minimized and especially the emotions of ordinary life are resented or rejected as themes of art. "Our most important thoughts are those which contradict our feelings," says Valéry repeatedly;[18] and, "All emotion, all sentiment indicates a defect in adaptation." Valéry resents the emotional effect of art: e.g., he complains that in reading Stendhal's *Lucien Leuwen* as a young man he felt the illusion so strongly that he could "no longer distinguish clearly between my own feelings and those which the artifice of the author communicated to me. . . . *Lucien Leuwen* brought about in me the miracle of a confusion which I detest." [19] We hardly need to say that Valéry has no use for confessional literature and looks very coldly at the criterion of "sincerity" or "good intention":

> Everything that aims at sensibility . . . romances, Musset, beggars, the poor of Victor Hugo, Jean Valjean arouses disgust if not anger in me. Pascal playing with death, Hugo with poverty, though they be virtuosos on their instruments, are basically repugnant to me. The calculated effort to draw tears, to break hearts, to excite by something too beautiful or too sad, makes me merciless. Emotion seems to me a forbidden means. It is an ignoble act to make anybody weak.[20]

Thus nothing seems to him more absurd than "to confide one's sorrow to paper. . . . What a quaint idea! That's the origin of many bad books, and of all the worst ones." The essay on Stendhal, though not without sympathy, sees him as an exploiter of sincerity. "The will to be sincere with oneself is inevitably a principle of falsification." Such an author is an actor who arrives at cynicism out of desperate ambition. "When we no longer know what to do in order to create a stir and to survive, we prostitute ourselves, we expose our *pudenda*, we offer them to public view." In telling the history of his return to poetry, Valéry somewhat ruefully admits that "the majority of writers have tried, and the greatest poets have miraculously succeeded in the task of reproducing the immediate emotions of life." But he always resented literature which tried to convert and persuade him. "I dislike picturing, across the page I read, a flushed or derisive face, on which is painted the intention to make me love what I hate or hate what I love." [21] This is the task of politics and eloquence but not of poetry and certainly not of the poetry Valéry wants to write. He wanted to go a different way and did so. He has a clear conception of a work of art constructed by the intellect, free from personal and emotional admixtures, pure, or as he sometimes says, absolute poetry.

The phrase *pure poetry*, old as such, is first used by Valéry in the Preface to Lucien Fabre's *Connaissance de la déesse* (1920) to suggest the ideal of the symbolists, which will always remain an ideal, though Valéry recognizes that it is only an abstract ideal. [22] It is a tendency toward the utmost rigor in art, "toward a beauty ever more conscious of its genesis, ever more independent of all *subjects*, and free from the vulgar attractions of sentiment as well as from the blatant effects of eloquence." It is "the perfect vacuum and the absolute zero of temperature—ideals neither of which can be attained, and only approached at the price of an exhausting series of efforts." It is "pure in the sense in which a physicist speaks of pure water." [23] Pure poetry is a "poetry which results, by a kind of *exhaustion*, from the progressive suppression of the prosaic elements of a poem. By prosaic elements we mean everything that *without damage* can be said also in prose; everything, history, legend, anecdote, morality, even philosophy, which exists by itself without the necessary co-operation of song." [24] The purity of poetry is obviously for Valéry a standard of judgment. "A poem is worth as much as it contains of pure poetry." At times, Valéry thinks of it as a kind of admixture of pure gold among foreign matter. "What one calls a poem is in practice composed of fragments of pure poetry embedded in the substance of a discourse." [25]

But what is this pure gold, how can it be distinguished from prose? Poetry, first of all, cannot be paraphrased, cannot be reduced to its prose content. Valéry condemns in strongest terms the heresy of paraphrase. "Nothing beautiful can be summarized. . . . Homer and Lucretius were not yet pure. Epic poets, didactic poets, and their like, are impure." The "absurd school exercise which consists of putting verse into prose . . . implies the belief that poetry is an *accident* of the *substance* prose. But poetry exists only for those in whose eyes such an operation is impossible and who recognize poetry by this very impossibility." The impossibility of paraphrase logically implies the impossibility of translating poetry. "Translations of the great foreign poets are architectural blueprints which may well be admirable; only they make the edifices themselves, palaces, temples, and the rest disappear . . . ." [26]

But why cannot poetry be reduced to prose, or to thought or theme? Valéry has several answers: one which he repeats many times is that prose language perishes when it is understood, while poetry demands repetition, demands and suggests a universe. Prose is practical, it presupposes a realm of ends. "As soon as the aim is reached, the word expires." But the universe of poetry is "a universe of reciprocal relations analogous to the universe of sounds within which the musical thought is born and moves. In this poetic universe, resonance triumphs over causality." The poem must "maintain itself in a condition as remote as possible from that of prose." "The poetic universe arises from the number, or rather from the density of images, figures, consonances, dissonances, by the linking of turns of speech and rhythms—the essential being continually to avoid anything that would lead back to prose." [27] Valéry here resumes old motifs of aesthetics: the contemplative isolation of poetry, its divorce from the world of ends, its creation of a new world that can be achieved only by exploiting the resources of language to the utmost, by removing its world from that of ordinary speech by use of sound and meter and all the devices of metaphorics.

Valéry stresses the poet's intimate relation to language: he has told several times the famous anecdote about Edgar Degas, who complained that he could not write although he was full of ideas for writing poetry, to which Mallarmé answered: "My dear Degas, poetry is not written with ideas. It is made with words." [28] For Valéry, the poet has a kind of "verbal materialism": "You know that only the words and the forms are the real discourse." Poets are combiners and arrangers of words. "One must adjust these complex words like irregular blocks, speculating about the chances and surprises which such arrangements prepare for us, and give the name of 'poets' to those whom fortune favors in this work." The real greatness of poets is that they are able to "grasp strongly with their words things of which they have had but fleeting glimpses in their minds." Literature, apparently all literature, "is in truth only a kind of speculation, a development of certain properties of language." The poet creates his own special language, a language within a language. "Like a political power [he] mints his own money." "The problem is how to extract from this practical instrument [everyday language] the means of realizing an essentially nonpractical work." [29]

If poetry is words, it is, of course, not words in isolation, but words in a pattern, words formalized. One could collect from Valéry the most extreme formalist statements. He quotes Frédéric Mistral with approval: "*There is nothing but form*

. . . form alone preserves the works of the mind." He approves
of Mallarmé, with whom "the material is no longer the *cause*
of the 'Form': it is one of the effects." Content is *"nothing
but an impure form*—that is to say a *confused* form." Valéry
praises Hugo because with him "the form is always master.
. . . Thought becomes with him a means and not the end of
expression." And he says of himself: "I subordinate 'content'
to 'form' (the nearer I am to my *best* state)—I am always in-
clined to sacrifice the *former* to the *latter*." [30]

Valéry complains that "the philosopher does not easily understand that the artist passes almost without distinction from
form to *content* as from *content* to *form*." The form, he says
with an inversion of usual imagery, is "the skeleton of works:
but some works have none. All works die, but those that have a
skeleton last much longer than those that were soft all through."
This formalism extends to the origin of the poem. "A delight-
ful, touching, 'profoundly human' (as the dunces say) idea
sometimes arises from the need to link up two stanzas, two de-
velopments of a theme." Once Valéry even said that "the prin-
cipal personages of a poem are always the smoothness and the
vigor of the verse." [31] But on the whole Valéry rarely goes to
such extremes of formalism, which could be matched only by
that of the Russian group.

Much more frequently Valéry thinks of poetry as a collab-
oration of sound and sense, a compromise between the two. He
conceives of sound and sense as "two independent variables,"
between which there is absolutely no relation. [32] Words are arbitrary signs: there is no natural relation between sound and
sense. The doctrine of the *mot juste* has no justification. "Flaubert was convinced that for every idea there exists a single
form. . . . This fine doctrine unfortunately makes no sense."
Thus the union of sound and sense established by the poet is
arbitrary but indissoluble: "The value of a poem resides in the
indissolubility of sound and sense. Now this is a condition
which seems to demand the impossible. There is no relation
between the sound and meaning of a word. . . . Yet is is the

business of the poet to give us the feeling of an intimate union between the word and the mind." This union must resist dissolution. "If the sense and the sound (or the content and the form) can be easily dissociated the poem *decomposes*." This union of sound and meaning is song, but not quite song. We must remember that Valéry also said that poetry is calculus, sport, exercise, even a game. But apparently song (*chant*) in Valéry's mind is not literally song (*carmen*); it is also enchantment, incantation, charm, magic. Valéry called a collection of his poems *Charmes*; and he means it also as a suggestion of the original function of poetry. "There is a very ancient man in every true poet; he still drinks from the very springs of language." But this primitivism is reconcilable with the greatest refinement. Mallarmé, "the least primitive of poets, gave . . . the magic formula." [33] The poet is the Orpheus who brings all nature to life,[34] who has the animizing power of ancient man. Thus all poetry will be and must be metaphorical. "The poet who multiplies figures is only rediscovering within himself language in its *nascent state*." [35]

Poetry is thus figurative and incantatory and, of course, metrical. Valéry has little use for free verse. He always praises the merits of strict metrical schemes and of all poetic conventions. "The demands of a strict prosody are the artifice that confers on natural language the qualities of a resistant matter." In verse, as Valéry interprets it, there must always be a clash between speech and metrical pattern and even the most artificial rules of French metrics are good (though arbitrary) just as any kind of restraint is good. Even a small vocabulary is considered a good thing: "A restricted vocabulary, from which one knows how to form numerous combinations, is worth more than thirty thousand words which do nothing but embarrass the acts of the mind." Valéry defends stanzaic forms and is enraptured by the sonnet. He would want to encounter its inventor in the underworld. However bad his sonnets might have been, Valéry would like to tell him: "I set you in my heart above all the poets of the earth and the underworld. . . . You have invented a *form*, and the greatest have accommodated themselves to this form." The constant argument is the value of convention, of restriction, even of chains. ":Restriction can be achieved only by the arbitrary." Valéry can thus revive one of the oldest doctrines of poetics, that of difficulties overcome. This "difficulty overcome" is for Valéry a criterion of value. "Every judgment which one wants to make of a work of art must first of all take into account the difficulties which the author has set up for himself to overcome." [36] We hardly need to say that Valéry prefers classicism to romanticism: classicism is superior because of its set conventions.

All these elaborate conventions, the dance, even the dance in fetters, are there for a purpose: to achieve that ideal artwork, unified, antirelative, nontemporal, imperishable, eternal, something beyond the decay of nature and man, something absolute. The poem, Valéry says, is "a closed system of all parts in which nothing can be modified." [37] Beauty, Valéry defines, is precisely "the sentiment of the impossibility of variation." "What is finished, what is complete gives us the feeling of our being powerless to modify it." "What is not entirely finished does not yet exist," he says paradoxically, especially in view of his constant insistence on poetry as an act, as a continuous activity and on the impossibility of finishing. But this is precisely the distant ideal of perfection for which Valéry finally has to give up finding words. Beauty is ultimately inexpressible. It implies an effect of ineffability, indescribability, it signifies "inexpressibility." "Literature attempts by words to create the state of a lack of words." Thus a central obscurity in poetry is justified. "What is clear and comprehensible and corresponds to a precise idea does not produce the effect of the divine." "Everything that is beautiful, generous, heroic is in essence obscure, incomprehensible. . . . Whoever swears faithfulness to clarity, renounces thereby being a hero." [38]

This curious criterion of resistance to transformation is very central to Valéry's ideal of poetry. Racine's *Phèdre*, he discovered, resisted attempts to change it. "I learned by direct experience and immediate sensation what is perfection in a work." [39] A lack of this resistance is what Valéry considers the main objection to the novel:

> As a reader of novels and histories I could not help observing all the freedom which these writings left me to modify [them] at my pleasure. . . . Novels demand passivity. They claim to make you take them at their word. They should be careful not to awaken the faculty of invention which, as to details, is in all of us at least equal to that of the author, and which can be, at every moment, exercised diabolically and can amuse itself with modifying the text, with bringing in an infinite number of possible substitutions which every narrative allows without noticeable alterations of its theme. . . . That is why I admire those novelists who tell us that they live (as one says) their characters and live them to the point of being rather lived by them than living them. I am convinced that they speak the truth as I myself have once or twice in my life experienced something analogous, I think, to such a sort of incarnation. But how can one gloss over the fact that everything ends on paper, that however intense and intimate the illusion of the author may be, it is translated into words, into phrases fixed once for all for everybody, exposed to our view, to the reactions and maneuvers of a mind which may be an active mind? [40]

Valéry can rewrite a novel, in imagination, and that is why it is "a naive genre," ultimately inferior to poetry. But this is not the only reason for Valéry's depreciation of the novel. The novel is also "historical," based on truth and memory, and neither truth nor memory means anything in art for Valéry. He does not care for memories. "I certainly shall not search for lost time," he says, alluding to his difference from Proust. Just as he does not care to remember his own past, so he does not care for history. "I am antihistorical," he says bluntly, and he often regrets the effects of historiography: the inciting of national passions, the keeping alive of old grievances and illusions. [41]

His other objection to the novel is its claim to "truth":

"Whereas the world of poetry is essentially closed and complete in itself, being purely a system of ornaments and accidents of language, the universe of the novel, even of the fantastic novel, is joined to the real world—just as a painted background merges imperceptibly into real objects, among which a spectator comes and goes." Valéry finds this appeal to truth puzzling. How is it that "a collection of details which are insignificant in themselves, and valueless one by one should produce a passionate interest and the impression of life?" "The novel," he says elsewhere, slightly varying the thought, "is possible because of the fact that this truth costs nothing . . . like air or sunlight. It lends itself to an infinity of compositions of equal probability." Besides, the novel is, of course, prose in Valéry's sense. "Unlike poems, a novel can be summarized; in other words, its plot can be told. It can be shortened without materially changing the story; . . . it can also be translated without losing its value. It can be developed internally and prolonged indefinitely." The same is true of epic poetry, of any long poem. It "can be summarized. . . . A melody cannot be summarized," says Valéry, crushingly to his mind, as statement and truth are excluded *a priori* from his definition of poetry.[42]

It is merely consistent that Valéry does not know what to do with drama although he himself wrote dramatic scenes, dialogues, and what he calls "mélodrames."[43] "Everything that is dramatic in life, in history, etc., seems to me of secondary interest. . . . This indifference to violent and spectacular incidents explains to me why I am not a novelist, a historian, or a dramatist."[44] He is frankly puzzled as to why man finds pleasure in tragedy. He recognizes that

man likes to feed on the sight of the misfortune of others. Two centuries ago, ladies went to see people put to torture. In any case it seems that the tragic genre is completely opposed to the production, in the soul, of the highest state which art can create

in it: the contemplative state—the state of sensuous knowledge
in which all the notions and emotions which cannot enter into
the composition of a harmonious, though momentary life are
abolished at the same time.[45]

Still, surprisingly, Valéry recognizes that Greek tragedy has
accomplished the impossible:

In putting on the stage the most atrocious stories in the world,
they have imposed upon them all the purity and perfection of a
form which insensibly communicates to the spectator of crimes
and evils an indefinable feeling which makes him regard these
horrible disorders with a divine eye. . . . [He can] always come
back from the emotion to comprehension, from excess to measure, from the exceptional to the norm, and from nature over-
thrown to the unchangeable presence of the profound order of
the world.[46]

One cannot help reflecting that Valéry might have admitted the
same transforming power of art in other cases: even in the epic
or the social novel, as he himself admits that there is, "in the
order of the arts, no theme and no model which execution cannot ennoble or degrade, make a cause of disgust or pretext for
enthusiasm." Actually, Valéry appreciated the poetic power of
Zola. But in his own practice he more and more insisted on
only one theme of poetry: that of "the life of intelligence
[which] constitutes an incomparable lyrical universe. . . .
There is an immense realm of the intellectual sensibility," hith-
erto neglected by poetry.[47] It was Valéry's right to insist on this
discovery; every artist recommends the art he himself prac-
tices. Every artist is an apologist for his own art, and that is, in
part, the interest of his criticism. But as a general theory of
literature it seems an extremely narrow, exclusive, puristic
view, a specialty hardly applicable beyond that unique closed
system of Valéry's civilized mind.

Valéry's ideal of poetry remains absolute, almost frozen into
the grandeur of a "pure form." One would imagine that such a
hard structure would have to be apprehended by its audience as
purely as it was conceived, as impersonally as it was created.

But here Valéry's strong sense of the discontinuity of author and reader interferes. A work of art to his mind is open to many interpretations, is only in a loose relationship to its audience. A work of art is essentially ambiguous. "It is an error contrary to the nature of poetry and which could even be fatal to it, to claim that to a poem corresponds one single, true meaning which conforms to or is identical with some thought of the author." [48] Valéry, with a sort of mischievous courtesy, has written introductions to Gustave Cohen's commentary on *Cimitière marin* and to Alain's commentaries on *Charmes*, which manage to praise the authors without committing himself to the acceptance of a single one of their interpretations. [49] "My verses have the meaning which one gives to them," he says bluntly. "There is no true sense of a text. The author has no authority. Whatever he wanted to say, he has written what he has written." The last part of this pronouncement is entirely defensible: it reasserts his suspicion of good intentions. "Bad verses are made of good intentions." Valéry is quite right to say, "when a work has appeared, its interpretation by the author has no more value than its interpretation by someone else. . . . My intention is only my intention and the work is the work." [50]

This insight into the detachment of the work from the author, into the "intentional fallacy," does not dispose of the problem of interpretation. All interpretations are not equal: there remains the problem of correctness. Valéry seems nearer the truth when he says: "There is no very fine work which is not susceptible of a great variety of equally plausible interpretations. The richness of a work is the number of senses or values which it can receive while still remaining itself." [51] The accretion of meaning in the process of history is a fact: great works of art have proved their vitality by this variety of appeal. Valéry recognizes the effects of history on the meaning of a work of art. "The change of an era, which is a change of reader, is comparable to a change in the text itself, a change which is always unforeseeable and incalculable." Valéry echoes a phrase used by Coleridge when he says that "certain works are created by their public. Certain other works create their public." [52] But Valéry indulges in dangerous paradoxes when he asserts the role of "creative misunderstanding" [53] or gives us this little dialogue: "I understand this text badly. . . . Don't bother. I find fine things. It draws them out of me. It matters little that I know what the author said. My error becomes the author." [54] Here the way would be opened to extreme caprice and anarchy. The break between work and audience would be complete.

But we must not make too much of irreconcilable contradictions and paradoxes in Valéry's thought. In discussing Descartes he has warned us that "every system is an enterprise of the mind against itself. . . . If one tries to reconstruct a thinking being from an examination of the texts alone, one is led to the invention of monsters who are incapable of life in direct proportion to the strict carefulness that one has devoted to the elaboration of the study." [55] We must not try to force unity on Valéry's thought, we must not invent a logical monster. Let us be content to have shown the main motifs of his thought on poetry.

Georg Lukács
(1885–1971)

Georg Lukács is the most important Marxist critic outside of Russia, except perhaps Walter Benjamin, who was a Marxist only late in his life and thus was affected by Marxism only in a small part of his work. The question of whether Lukács can be described as an orthodox expounder of Marxist theory is a moot one: in 1968 a book of collected articles from Hungary and East Germany elaborately attacked him for "revisionism."[1] In 1956 Lukács was for a short time Minister of Culture in the Hungarian government of Imre Nagy. After the suppression of the Hungarian revolt by Russian tanks, Lukács was deported to Rumania but was allowed to return to Budapest in April 1957. After that he lived in retirement on a government pension but was able to publish books in West Germany. After Khrushchev's exposure of Stalin's crimes, Lukács joined in strongly condemning the purges and the terror and praised Solzhenitzyn's books in special essays.

There is, however, no doubt of Lukács's total commitment to Marxism-Leninism since the end of World War I. His early writings during his years in Germany, in Heidelberg, *The Soul and the Forms* (1911) and *Theory of the Novel* (1916; in book form in 1920) were repudiated by him later in the strongest terms as "reactionary, full of idealistic mysticism."[2] They would demand extensive discussion on their own right which I shall forego on this occasion. I may just remark that *The Soul and the Forms* expounds a highly aesthetic and somewhat existentialist view of tragedy: "Tragedy has only one dimension: that of height. It occurs at the moment when mysterious forces extract his essence from man, reduce him to the essential."[3] The first essay in the volume defends criticism as an intermediate form between creation and systematic philosophy. One feels the neighborhood of German *Lebensphilosophie*. *Theory of the Novel* is much more speculative, even Hegelian in its assumptions. It elaborates a scheme according to which the epic, in practice Homer, reflected the original totality of life, a harmony of objectivity, while the modern novel depicts rather the conflict between individual aspiration and the objective world. It is a curious variation of Schiller's contrast between naive and sentimental poetry.

The question of a continuity between the early Lukács and his later Marxist period would deserve careful investigation. There is no doubt a clear break between the two periods, but on the other hand one can argue, as Peter Demetz has done persuasively, that some central, permanent convictions remain unaltered throughout his long career: the dichotomy of content and form with priority given to content, the concept of type, and the triadic scheme of history. Demetz speaks of a "renaissance of an originally idealistic aesthetics in the mask of Marxism,"[4] a formula I would not endorse as it seems to suggest that Lukács's Marxism was a disguise, a put-on. But Demetz is surely right in emphasizing the sources of Lukács's aesthetic in Germany: in Hegel primarily, but also in Goethe and Schiller. To these we must add the Russian radical critics: Vissarion Belinsky, Nikolai Chernyshevsky, and Nikolai Dobrolyubov, who in turn owe much to the German tradition, Belinsky in particular. And then there are of course Marx and Engels. Lukács has written so much on the history of aesthetics that it is not difficult to demonstrate these relationships. He wrote on Aristotle, then jumped to Lessing, Goethe, Schiller, Hegel, F. T. Vischer, and the Russian critics. A study of the literary theories of Marx and Engels tries to extract as much as possible from their casual pronouncements.[5] Lukács's political and ideological commitment to Marxism came about late in World War I when Lukács joined the Hungarian Communist party, thus repudiating his own banker family and their "nobility" (he had himself used the form: Georg von Lukács) and opposing the Hungarian feudal aristocracy which was then in control of the government. He took part as Deputy Commissar of Education and Culture in Béla Kun's short-lived Hungarian Communist regime in 1919. He then had to flee to Vienna and later to Berlin and was completely involved in politics. Only in 1931 did Lukács return to anything that could be called literary criticism and aesthetics, after books such as *History and Class-Consciousness* (1923), a small book on *Lenin* (1924), and many political articles. The contributions to a Berlin periodical *Linkskurve* (1931–32) consistently refer to "our" proletarian literature and develop, often polemically, Lukács's main doctrines which he held tenaciously for the rest of his life. Only late in his life did he systematize them in the treatise *On Specificity as a Category of Aesthetics* (1967, but using articles published in 1954–55), and in *Aesthetik* (2 vol., 1963). These bulky theoretical books draw conclusions from Lukács's many volumes on the problems of realism, on *Russian Realism* (1949), on the *Historical Novel* (1955), on *Goethe and His Age* (1947), and on the *German Realists of the Nineteenth Century* (1951), as well as the smaller tracts on *Balzac* (1952) and on *Thomas Mann* (1949, expanded 1953) and general sketches of the history of German literature (1945, expanded 1953), not to speak of small pamphlets and scattered articles on topics ranging from Lessing to Kafka. I can only allude to his detailed study of the *Young Hegel* (1948) and a harsh criticism of German nineteenth-century philosophy, called *The Destruction of Reason* (1954).[6]

For our limited purposes it will be best to ignore the shifts in Lukács's later views, partly due to the sinuosities of the party line which he felt compelled or was compelled to follow and to concentrate on his main ideas which remained remarkably consistent. Lukács starts from the basic conviction of Marxist materialism: i.e., that there is an objective reality totally independent of man's mind and that this Being determines Consciousness. This is a frequently repeated quotation from Marx and Engels' *Deutsche Ideologie* (1845–46): "It is not the consciousness of men which determines their being, but, on the contrary, their social being which determines their consciousness." Literature is thus conceived as part of the "superstructure," as a reflection of the objective social reality. "*Widerspiegelung der Wirklichkeit*" (reflection of reality) is Lukács's obsessive central metaphor. In the first volume of the *Aesthetik* the phrase is repeated (I counted) 1,032 times. I was too bored to count it in volume 2. *Widerspiegelung* comes, in Lukács, from Lenin's use of *odrazhenie* (reflection) and ultimately descends from the neo-Platonic tradition. We all know that Hamlet spoke of art "holding up the mirror to nature," and that Stendhal said the novel is "a mirror dawdling down the road." Taken literally, the image is surely misleading. Literature is not a mirror of society if mirror means reflection, in exact proportions, nor is it a good image if it means a reverse reflection, flattened out and somewhat dimmer than the original. Lukács, however, clings to this image throughout his writings, though in the *Aesthetik* he explains at great length that "reflection" is not to be conceived of as "mechanical, photographical reproduction," and he admits that in art there is an "inevitable subjective component." Much of the *Aesthetik* is concerned with an attempt to define the "specificity" as the aesthetic category in difference from the scientific category of generality and the everyday category of particularity. Lukács admits even that "what in every other sector (*Gebiet*) of human life would be philosophical idealism, i.e., that no object can exist without a subject, is in the aesthetic an essential trait of its specific objectivity (*Gegenständlichkeit*)."[7] Let us forget about the awkward metaphor of mirroring. Lukács really uses the term as a substitute for *mimesis*, representation, and in his later *Aesthetik* appeals expressly to Aristotle for the distinction between mimesis and deception or illusion. As I am primarily concerned with literature, I shall not follow Lukács in his tortuous attempts to make music and architecture mirror reality. Mimesis is certainly one aspect of the literary transaction and we can accept the view that literature somehow represents reality and social reality in particular.

This representation is, however, conceived by Lukács in a very specific way which gives the old concept of mimesis a new meaning. Literature not only represents social reality but *should* represent the very structure of society, provide an insight into its organization, and, with this insight, a feeling for the direction of its development, a prophetic sense of its future, which is defined as socialism, or rather communism. Thus the contemporary writer is asked to depict reality as it is, objectively, realistically, but with his mind on the future society, socialistically, propagandistically. The obvious contradiction does not bother Lukács and other Marxists. The writer in the prerevolutionary past is asked the same question: Does he have insight into the structure of society and its movement? Does he believe in progress, that defined as progress toward socialism and in the more distant past, progress from feudalism toward the bourgeois rule, toward capitalism? But this insight into the movement of society need not, Lukács argues insistently, be a rational knowledge or a consciously held belief in the future of socialism. It can and may be demonstrated simply by the writer's power of depicting his society truthfully even if his consciously professed political views were opposed to progress. Lukács' prize examples are Walter Scott and Balzac. The conservative views of both of these authors cannot be ignored. Scott was a Tory, Balzac a royalist, but, according to Lukács, both saw deeply into the structure of their societies: saw, in Scotland, the struggle between the classes at the crucial historical crises, or in France predicted the victory of the bourgeoisie over feudalism. This view of the contradiction between conscious and unconscious intentions is not new: the Schlegels were, for instance, quite aware that conscious intentions might be irrelevant. Dobrolyubov, in the 1860s, thought of social types as revealing an author's world-view independently of or even contrary to his conscious intentions. Gogol is his stock example. Gogol was a reactionary but his work predicts the decay of the Tsarist system and the feudal society. There is, of course, the famous letter, in English, by Engels, dating from 1888, which argues that Balzac was "compelled to go against his own class sympathies and political prejudices" as he "saw the real men of the future where for the time being they alone were to be found—that I consider one of the greatest triumphs of Realism." [8] With Lukács this contrast becomes a major preoccupation. He finds such clashes between work and conscious intention throughout history and considers one of the main functions of criticism this uncovering of the hidden meanings and sympathies implied in an author's work. As D. H. Lawrence said succinctly: "Never trust the writer, trust the tale." [9]

Lukács can succeed because he looks at a work of art as a totality which should reflect the totality of society. The work of art is made up of people, of characters engaged in an action. They are discussed and analyzed as if they were real people, though Lukács knows, in theory, the difference between fiction and life and knows that books are invented by men. When the awkward question is raised, why in a certain time the historical situation is mirrored very differently by different works, the author's biographical vicissitudes, his talents, and his morals are called upon to account for the differences. But the standard is always that of a presumably accurate mirror of the social reality at a specific time by which an author is judged.

In this criticism, the fictional figures do not exist in a vacuum of art for art's sake, as parts of an imaginary world, but only as "images" to be studied for their correspondences to reality and their anticipations of the future. Lukács, unlike many Marxists, is not concerned with the social origins of a writer. He has no use for what he calls "vulgar sociologism," which,

e.g., reduces a writer to a spokesman of a specific group—
Gogol, the typical Ukrainian landowner of the early nineteenth
century—as he considers the conversion to Marxism, the identification with the proletariat, more important than class origins. He must defend his own way to Marxism since he was the
son of a prosperous Jewish banker who was given a title of
lower nobility, even though this emphasis on a profession of
faith contradicts his conviction about the irrelevance of intentions. But, of course, the mere profession of faith does not, in
Lukács's view, exempt a writer from being criticized for his
lack of insight into the structure of society or his power to em-
body this insight in convincing figures and actions. Some of
Lukács's earliest literary criticism in the Marxist vein consists
of sharp criticisms of German proletarian novels by Willy Bre-
del and Ernst Ottwalt (the latter, incidentally, a victim of the
purges in 1936) which were good Communist propaganda,[10]
but only propaganda, according to Lukács, and did not succeed
in creating images, totalities, genuine works of art. Similarly,
Lukács often criticized Soviet literature for good intentions,
for mere abstract statements and exhortations. For Lukács a
great work must be a totality, that is, a unity of form and content, of subjectivity and objectivity, with priority always given
to content as the objective world must have preference before
the subjective. "Form problems are determined by the problems of content," he says over and over again. As early as 1909
(when he was twenty-four) he could write "specific world-
views bring specific forms with them."[11]

What matters in a work of art is the proper balance between
universality and particularity which Lukács calls "specificity": something like Hegel's "concrete universal." Success in
achieving it is demonstrated for Lukács mainly by the writer's
creation of types. The type is Lukács's main interest, it is to
him "one of the central problems of aesthetics."[12] It is the justification of literature as man's image of himself. The type is
neither the average nor the eccentric. It is, to quote one of his
formal definitions, "the innermost essence of a personality as

moved and defined by such determinations which belong objectively to a significant tendency of the evolution of society." [13] The type, Lukács emphasizes, must not be isolated
from the total work. He condemns the literature on Hamlet,
Faust, Don Quixote, and Madame Bovary as characters apart
from their context. [14] The typical figure must be seen in action,
within the total work of art. The work of art must be animated
by a point of view, a specific world view, a perspective, must
be "partial," a term which, in Lukács, shifts easily from the
necessarily engaged, committed, or simply sympathetic or sa-
tirical view of an author to the party spirit, the *partijnost* in
Lenin's sense. (One should note—and Lukács knows this [15]—
that Lenin's famous article, dated November 1905, requires
loyalty, party spirit, only from members of the party and concerns party literature. It expressly grants others the right to
write and talk as they please.)

Usually Lukács asks for a world view. A characterization,
he argues, "cannot be complete which does not include the
world view of a character." One of the functions of the critic is
is to determine whether "the artist succeeded in uncovering the
manifold connections between the individual traits of his heroes and the objective general problems of the age." [16] Not only
is the character examined for his world view but also the author
is asked to have "a firm and vital world view." [17] It need not
necessarily be a world view Lukács approves of. He seems not
to be worried by the example of Tolstoy who, he says, "on the
basis of a completely false world view produced immortal
masterpieces." [18] Lukács does not mind the contradiction between conscious intention and creation and can, e.g., say that
"Gogol's writings have an objective revolutionary character" [19]
though he knows, of course, that Gogol was a defender of tsar-
dom and orthodoxy. Thus the value of a writer rests on the
creation of prophetic social types such as Gorky's Mother or
Heinrich Mann's Untertan, not in correct political foresight. [20]
Types thus fulfill an important social function: they present us
with models of behavior, with ideals to live up to. Soviet Rus-

sian literature is totally committed to this view of the positive hero, and it would be foolish to deny that certain literary figures have exerted this role of models throughout history; the knights of medieval romances, the monks of saints' lives, Hamlet, and Werther are obvious examples. But one may doubt whether the role of literature should be confined to this creation of types and whether types are necessarily the highest artistic achievements. In Italy, the fine critic and historian Francesco De Sanctis has attacked the emphasis on types and has argued, persuasively to my mind, that types, when socially effective, are actually deprived of their concrete aesthetic value. Achilles becomes wrath, Thersites meanness, Odysseus slyness, Don Quixote foolish fancy, Hamlet hesitation and indecision, Faust striving, etc. The figures are allegorized, lose their specificity, and hence their value as successful art.[21]

It follows from this whole view that all good literature is realistic. It mirrors society, it is "thinking in images" about the evolution of mankind, about social development. Realism, says Lukács, is not a "style" but "the basis of every literature."[22] It is by no means confined to what historically has been called realism. Shakespeare, Goethe, even Homer and Dante are called "realists" and a defense of devices which we would call "fantastic" is not uncommon in Lukács as long as these techniques are made to serve as means of representing reality truthfully,[23] accurately, correctly. Thus Lukács approves of extreme situations depicted in literature if they present "a total picture of the changing order, of the revealed law of the world."[24] He can defend the chance encounters and other improbabilities in *Père Goriot*[25] and in *War and Peace*.[26] Lukács even approves of E. T. A. Hoffmann, since he assumes that he "represents some deeper reality in fantastic garb." His work is "an image of the transition of Germany from the distortion of feudal absolutism to a distorted capitalism."[27] He calls him even "a really great realist."[28]

While, in theory, Lukács's concept of realism is extremely broad and would seem to allow almost any kind of art, in prac-

tice, he makes nineteenth-century realism the standard of literature. Balzac and Tolstoy are his heroes, and by their standards
later literature is accepted, measured, and condemned. Much
of Lukács's most satisfying writing is devoted to the classics of
nineteenth-century realism. Particularly, the book on Russian
realism contains two essays on Tolstoy which are perceptive in
setting Tolstoy in his time and in relation to Western literature
though Lukács accepts and develops, too uncritically to my
mind, Lenin's view that Tolstoy somehow represents the peas-
ants' revolt.[29] He thus grossly overrates *The Resurrection*. The
essay on Dostoevsky, short and skimpy, almost ignores the late
great novels and makes the Dostoevsky of *Crime and Punish-
ment* and earlier work the champion of the insulted and injured:
a plebeian revolutionary in spite of his conservative convictions.[30]

The attitude toward the German classics is much more ambiguous. Lukács admires Goethe immeasurably and tries to
see him as a realist, even as an instinctive materialist. The
main thesis of *Goethe and His Age* (1947) is directed polemically against those who see Goethe in conflict with the En-
lightenment. Goethe, he argues, is rather its culmination in
Germany. Lukács, contrary to all evidence, minimizes Goethe's hostility to the French revolution and sees everywhere
proofs of "enlightened sympathies with the ideals of the
French revolution" in the Germany of Goethe's time. This is
rather easy to show with Schiller, but Lukács makes an attempt
to claim Hölderlin as a Jacobin, a thesis which has since been
elaborated by Pierre Bertaux but cannot be proved convincingly.[31] Still all the great Germans of the classical age are used
by Lukács to contrast the realm of thoughts and dreams with
the German political *misère*. With the exception of Goethe,
they remained abstract, idealistic, alienated, and hence socially ineffectual.

All literature after nineteenth-century realism is judged as a
kind of retrogression. Lukács distinguishes two trends in post-
realistic literature: naturalism and decadence equated with the

avant-garde or with formalism. The criticism of naturalism is based on Lukács's condemnation of description in comparison to narration. Zola's description of the horse race in *Nana* is skillfully contrasted with the horse race in *Anna Karenina*.[32] Description means stasis, inertia, lack of selectivity, preponderance of mere matter, abstract objectivity. The mirror of art is too wide. Zola and Gerhart Hauptmann were Lukács's main targets, but naturalism is considered more widely as a debilitating trait of much "modernist" literature. At times it seems that Lukács considers all modern literature a version of naturalism, lacking in a proper hierarchy of values, conceived of as anarchy. The overwhelming power of the milieu in early naturalism, the preponderance of mere mood in impressionism and symbolism, the *montage* of raw pieces of reality in the movement called *Neue Sachlichkeit*, the stream of association in surrealism are all considered forms of naturalism.[33] Even Joyce and his technique of the interior monologue is considered a version of naturalism. Lukács draws an elaborate comparison between Molly's concluding monologue in *Ulysses* and the monologue put into the mouth of Goethe in Thomas Mann's *Lotte in Weimar*. In Mann's novel, Lukács argues, the interior monologue is merely a technical device; in Joyce it shows a cleaving to the surface of life, to the fleeting moment. It is an expression of a lack of aim and purpose, of mere neutrality, of inactivity (*Zuständlichkeit*).[34]

Lukács's polemics, especially in later years when the menace of naturalism had ceased to be an urgent issue, were directed against all "modernist" literature. The attack is sweeping and all-inclusive: symbolism, expressionism, surrealism, etc., are all condemned, and no figure in Western literature finds Lukács's approval unless he can be viewed as resuming the great tradition of nineteenth-century realism. Thomas Mann is for him the exemplary late bourgeois. On occasion Lukács also praises other survivors from nineteenth-century realism— Romain Rolland, Roger Martin du Gard—and in late years he made a few favorable references to Thomas Wolfe.[35] In his book

The Historical Novel (in Russian, 1938; in German, 1954), Lukács hailed some of the German emigré writers who seemed to promise a revival of the historical novel and were committed to the Left. Heinrich Mann's novel on Henry IV of France, Arnold Zweig, and Lion Feuchtwanger are praised. The Preface to the 1954 edition confesses some disenchantment with these authors or rather with the hopes that Lukács had put on them.

Lukács's main polemics are directed against avant-garde art, against any and all modernisms, not only naturalism. He conceives of the avant-garde mainly as an expression of nihilism, of existential anguish, *Angst*. Kafka is singled out in contrast to Thomas Mann. He is the classic of "stopping at the blind fear before reality." [36] He is—whether he admits it or not—an atheist whose God is Nothing: *Atheos absconditus*. The concrete type is replaced by abstract particularity, the poetic unity is broken up.[37] The world appears as an "allegory of a transcendent Nothing." Even his superbly realized details are "ciphers of a merely incomprehensible other world." The question of modern art is always put in the simplest alternatives: health vs. sickness, reason vs. unreason, optimism vs. pessimism, peace vs. war, confidence or hope vs. fear or anguish. Every work of art which shows anxiety is supposed to have an objective tendency leading either to Hitlerism or to the atomic war. In 1957 Lukács stated bluntly that all avant-garde art is "unartistic, even anti-artistic." [38]

It is hardly necessary to assemble Lukács's pronouncements on individual authors or movements. The famous paper condemning German expressionism as a forerunner of Nazism dates, one should realize, from 1934, when Gottfried Benn's siding with Nazism was in the news.[39] But the paper is not confined to this particular situation: it sees expressionism as solipsism, as idealism (a word which has a pejorative sense in the East). The abstract pacifism of the expressionists parallels the policy of the German Independent Socialist party which Lukács sees as an ineffectual compromise to the detriment of communism. A note, dated 1953, expressly asserts that the

Nazis' later condemnation of expressionism as "degenerate art" does not change the correctness of Lukács's analysis.[40]

I can only allude to Lukács's unfavorable view of the early Bertolt Brecht, who seemed to him an abstract propagandist using all the techniques of the avant-garde. In 1934 Lukács disapproved of the "epic theater," since he always believed in strictly defined genres: he rejected the *Verfremdungseffekt* as anti-Aristotelian, as unrealistic.[41] Brecht, then in exile in Denmark, was greatly upset by these criticisms but did not react in public.[42] Lukács much later retracted this judgment of Brecht by pleading ignorance of his more recent plays, *The Good Woman of Setzuan*, *Mother Courage*, etc.[43] After Brecht's death in 1956, Lukács spoke at a memorial occasion in Berlin praising him as "a genuine dramatist" and annexed him to "socialist realism" without retracting his criticism of the early Brecht or of his dramatic theories.[44]

The condemnation of all modernist literature is so sweeping that it would be otiose to give further examples. Rilke, for instance, is considered a decadent solipsist and is accused of "bestiality"[45] because he relates in a poem on the Swedish King Charles XII (in *Das Buch der Bilder*) that the king captured girls in the Ukraine and had their bridegrooms hunted to death by dogs. Lukács comments that this idea could come from Goering. Similarly ignoring the dramatic context, Lukács used the famous poem on the panther as a lament about the abandonment of man and his loss of the world as if the panther were a man and Rilke were behind the bars of a cage.[46] The case of Rilke demonstrates what must be obvious to any reader of Lukács: his insensitivity to poetry and his helplessness in the face of the problem of the lyric. In the *Aesthetik* he makes an effort to assimilate the lyric to mimesis by arguing that "rhythm is a reflection of objective reality" as it originally arose from the rhythms of labor. He angrily criticizes the English Marxist Christopher Caudwell for exempting (in *Illusion and Reality*) the lyric from the social world and relegating it to a world of dreams related to magic.[47] In discussing Eichendorff, Lukács expresses some understanding for his simple melancholy, for his sense of man's solitude, but immediately allegorizes it as a picture of the Germany of his time and a reflection of Eichendorff's easily ascertainable ideology. He was a Catholic landowner who yearned for a vanished past. *Aus dem Leben eines Taugenichts* (*Memoirs of a Good-for-Nothing*) is interpreted as a revolt against capitalism: its division of labor, its enslavement of man. We are treated to a quotation from Marx on the desirability of shortening the workday and a disquisition on the importance of leisure time.[48]

Lukács is almost exclusively interested in the novel and drama as they allow a discussion of characters and actions, of social pictures and ideologies. Lukács is a firm believer in the division of genres and even in the need for preserving their purity. He constantly works with their differences and judges by *genre* criteria. The novel (as he had argued in his early book, *The Theory of the Novel*) searches for the totality of life: hence the quest of the hero, his "education," which became Lukács's main concern. The German *Bildungsroman* centers on the hero, Wilhelm Meister, and Goethe's novel is, in Lukács's view, the one work which most successfully reconciles particularity with universality, though its humanism has still an escapist character.[49] The group of active men, the Society of the Tower, remains an "island" in its time. The line to Gottfried Keller's *Der grüne Heinrich* and to Thomas Mann is obvious. Everyone of Thomas Mann's books—*Buddenbrooks*, *The Magic Mountain*, and *Dr. Faustus*—is allegorized to become an analogue of the German history of its time. *Dr. Faustus*, in particular, lends itself to such a reading. Even *Death in Venice* is seen as signaling a barbaric underworld amidst European civilization somehow anticipating the menace of Nazism,[50] a view oddly enough accepted by Mann, who could not have thought of the homosexual seduction represented by Tadzio at that time as simply "barbaric."[51]

A second strand of the novel is the historical novel, which is the theme of a special book by Lukács.[52] The rise of the historical novel is tied to the upheavals of the French revolution and the Napoleonic wars. It is no chance that the first historical novel, Scott's *Waverley* was published in 1814. Scott, Lukács argues, was a great realist, and not a romantic, who seized on the crucial turning points of English (and Scottish) history; Scott depicts with epic grandeur and impartiality the conflict of classes, the life of the people, the "objective dialectics of a specific historical crisis."[53] Strikingly, Lukács defends the colorless hero of Scott's novels as the right "middle" figure which allows the novelist to see things with the eyes of the people. Only out of a careful picture of everyday life arise such historically important figures as Richard the Lionhearted, Louis XI of France, Queen Elizabeth, Mary Queen of Scots, and Cromwell, as fully developed heroes with a convincing romantic halo.

Scott's followers are discussed in their setting: Cooper in the United States, Pushkin in Russia, Manzoni in Italy. After 1848 the historical novel declines, according to Lukács. The organic link between past and present which was the secret of Scott and his followers was lost. Flaubert is seen as establishing a falsely antiquarian, exotic, private genre with *Salammbô*. Conrad Ferdinand Meyer is charged with having presented a decorative caricature of the decline of German democracy. Adalbert Stifter is seen as an escapist reactionary; Zola as an antirealist historian of the Second Empire, fantastic and grotesque in his distortions; Lukács sees, however, a revival of the historical novel in the works of Anatole France, Romain Rolland, Heinrich Mann, and Arnold Zweig.

Everywhere the novel is contrasted with the drama. The novel is epic, the drama aims at a convergence of characters and at a collision. Lukács appeals to Hegel's distinction between the epic as a "totality of objects" while drama produces a "totality of movement" in order to explain, rather tortuously, why there was a historical tragedy, in Shakespeare in particular, long before there was a historical novel.

Lukács often judges shrewdly—he sees social implications,

and he is good at unmasking hidden ideologies, but he seems to me often to fail badly in recognizing aesthetic differences and in grasping critical problems. He grossly overrates Scott as an artist (whatever his historical importance), and he over-praises such a poor Homeric or rather Ossianic *pastiche* as Gogol's *Taras Bulba*. On the other hand, he severely judges Conrad Ferdinand Meyer, a Swiss, merely for his professed sympathies for Bismarck and his detachment from the people, and he labels Stifter a philistine and reactionary contrary to all the evidence of his writings and biography (he committed sui-cide by cutting his throat). Lukács's unjust view of Stifter is surely influenced by the fact that Nietzsche praised him (Nie-tzsche is Lukács's *bête noire*), and by Ernst Bertram and other glorifiers of the German Biedermeier period who are labeled "fascist" or *fascisierend*.[54]

The purely ideological, politically polemical character of much of Lukács's criticism is obvious in his exaltation of "so-cialist realism," the only alternative to decadence in our time. Socialist realism is supposed to be qualitatively on a higher level than any preceding literature: it is "an historically con-ditioned artistic superiority,"[55] which follows from its accurate knowledge of the future of mankind: i.e., the victory of com-munism. At the same time, Lukács criticized what he consid-ers the survival of bourgeois mentality in Soviet Russia and is extremely niggardly in dispensing praise to specific Soviet works: only Mikhail Sholokhov and A. S. Makarenko are treated in some detail and, e.g., in the Preface to the *Historical Novel* (1938) Lukács pleads an unlikely surprising ignorance of Russian as excuse for not treating the current Russian histor-ical novel. After the lifting of the Stalinist terror Lukács praised Solzhenitzyn very highly: not only *One Day in the Life of Ivan Denisovich* (1964) but also *Cancer Ward* (1968) and *The First Circle*, (1968), suppressed in the East. The two novels repre-sent for him "the provisional summit of contemporary world literature." Much is made of Solzhenitzyn's technique of col-lecting, as in the *Magic Mountain*, people under stress in one place. The epic quality, that is, the totality, is supposedly preserved though the scenes are discontinuous and the characters often schematic. Solzhenitzyn is praised for his "plebeian" revolt against injustice but criticized for lacking a socialist perspective. Still, Lukács sees him as signifying a "rebirth of the noble beginnings of socialist realism."[56]

Lukács until his death clung to an ideology which seems more and more Utopian: a vision of a social paradise, of the end of the alienation of man for which there is no evidence in any Communist or other society. As a character in *The First Circle* remarks: "if you always look over your shoulder how can you still remain a human being?" Lukács looked or had to look over his shoulder all his adult life and found solace only in a distant Messianic hope.

Still it would be a mistake to underrate the enormous synthetic effort of the two-volume *Aesthetik*. Much of it rehearses old ideas: "the identity of form and content, the unity of essence and appearance, universality and intensive infinity of the content, of art as criticism of life, cathartic transformation of the whole man."[51] We hear again in detail about the historicity of art as a mirror of reality, the role of the type in literature, and so forth. What is new is the expansion of Lukács's ideas to the other arts: to music, painting, architecture, and the film, and the elaboration of the view that the arts arose independently of each other and conflated only much later in the historical process. New, though hardly surprising, is Lukács's emphasis on art as radically secular, anthropomorphizing. A whole long section[58] discusses the liberation of art from religion, its emancipation from any transcendence which for Lukács was, from the very beginning, a misunderstanding. Once he admits that the enormous flowering of medieval art "presents a real problem,"[59] but he brushes it aside by discussing the emergence of secular feelings and motifs within the religious framework of the Middle Ages. Also new is the use of Pavlov's signal systems, a gesture toward behaviorism which I find incomprehensible and even superfluous. It amounts to lit-

tle if art is described as an objectivization of the signal system
1 (that is, sensations, conditioned reflexes), to become supposedly a new signal system 1 in order to point out the difference from signal system 2 (i.e., concepts, science). Lukács
here merely translates his old ideas into a new terminology.
Naturalism, we are told, is either conditioned reflexes (i.e.,
undigested observation, signal system 1), or signal system 2
(theories, concepts, abstractions).[60] Lukács merely said that
Naturalism is either brute sensation or abstract thought, while
true realistic art is neither. Most interestingly, Lukács revives
Aristotle's *catharsis* as the right description of the effect of art.
But, catharsis is not conceived of as the purging of specific
emotions, pity and fear, as it is in Aristotle, but much more
generally as the "convulsion" (*Erschütterung*) of the whole
man. Art is able to influence man in a direction which helps or
hinders the formation of desirable human types.[61] Lukács sees
this always as an ethical and political problem which is still the
"kernel" of aesthetic experience. Stalin's view that artists and
writers are "engineers of the soul" is considered too narrow as
it makes art subservient to practical day-by-day tasks. Art cannot resign its claim to universality. Art is "*vox humana*"; it
expresses the truth of the historical moment for the life of
man."[62] One can accept this, whatever one may think of the
doctrinaire limitations of Lukács's humanism.

Roman Ingarden
(1893–1970)

Roman Ingarden was a Polish philosopher who, to my mind, made important contributions to a coherent theory of literature. I find myself in wide agreement with his views and acknowledge learning from him, on many of these questions, more than from anybody else. I shall voice some reservations and misgivings but nonetheless find that he clarified such questions as the mode of existence of a literary work of art, its multilayered structure, and the way we experience it, more clearly and acutely than any other aesthetician I know. Much of Ingarden's argumentation is couched in the language of phenomenology of his teacher in Göttingen and Freiburg, Edmund Husserl (1859–1938), and would require a disproportionate amount of time and effort to expound in all its intricacy. I shall have to be content with some simplification. But the technicality of Ingarden's language is not, I believe, the only reason for his slow penetration abroad: his first book, *The Literary Work of Art* (1931), the only book of his I knew in earlier years, was published just a year or so before the Nazi assumption of power in Germany.[1]

Ingarden as a Pole and Husserl as a Jew were ignored. A well-known German literary historian, Günther Müller, who in 1939 expounded some of Ingarden's views, did not even dare

or want to use the term *phenomenology* or to mention its origi-
nator, Husserl.[2] In 1937 Ingarden published, in Polish, a second book, *On the Cognition of a Literary Work of Art*, which
appeared, in a greatly expanded version, in German only in
1968.[3] In the meantime, Ingarden had undergone the persecu-
tion by the Nazis of the whole intellectual life of Poland during
the war, and he was shoved aside by the new Communist regime, which propounded historical materialism as its creed.
We must, I think, understand Ingarden's bitterness and feeling
of neglect by the circumstances of the time. Only in the very
last years of his life was he able to bring out a third and fourth
book in German, *Investigations in the Ontology of Art* (1962),
and *Experience, Work of Art, and Value* (1969). Posthumously
a small collection of articles of special interest for students of
literature appeared as *The Object and Tasks of Literary Scholarship* (1976).[4] Only in 1973 did the two basic books, *The Literary Work of Art* and *On the Cognition of a Literary Work of
Art*, appear in English translation.[5] But one has to know Polish
to study his many scattered writings available only in his mother tongue. I was, I believe, the first person to draw attention to
his work in English, first in a paper, "The Theory of Literary
History" (1936), published in the *Travaux* of the Linguistic
Circle in Prague; then in *Literary Scholarship: Its Aims and
Methods*, edited by Norman Foerster (1941); in a paper, "The
Mode of Existence of a Literary Work" (1942), which appeared in the last number of the old *Southern Review* and was
reprinted in widely used anthologies such as R. W. Stallman's
Critiques and Essays in Criticism (1949); and finally in *Theory
of Literature* (1949), which reprinted the 1942 paper almost
unchanged.[6]

How far my exposition of Ingarden has affected other critics
and aestheticians seems difficult to ascertain. I have the impression that my references to the Russian Formalists, to the
Czech Structuralists, and to Ingarden were simply put down as
evidences of my erudition, while *Theory of Literature* was
mistakenly, I think, considered a codification of the New Crit-

icism. I object to this view, as I came to this country with my theories fully formulated before I knew anything of the New Criticism. Here I shall focus on Ingarden's contribution to literary theory and will have to neglect his many papers and analyses of the other arts and his strictly philosophical writings.

The Literary Work of Art starts with a refutation of current concepts of the mode of existence of a literary work of art, mainly directed against "psychologism," i.e., the view that a work can be reduced to events in the mind of either the author or the reader. Ingarden concludes that a literary work of art is neither an ideal object such as a triangle nor a real object or artifact such as a statue or a picture. It cannot be a real object, as it is not made up of paper and blotches of ink but of sentences written or pronounced. Nor is it an ideal object such as a number or a triangle, as it originates at a specific time and may perish. It is what phenomenology terms an "intentional object," i.e., created by a specific person directed at a specific object. These distinctions, one should realize, have with Ingarden a philosophical purpose. He tried in an enormous two-volume work, *The Debate over the Existence of the World* (1947–48), to refute the transcendental idealism of his teacher Husserl while still preserving the phenomenological method.[7] By denying that the literary work is either a physical fact or an ideal object or an object in the consciousness of an individual, Ingarden can argue that the "author, with all his vicissitudes, experiences, and psychic states, remains completely outside the literary work."[8] And so does the reader, of course. No qualities, experiences, or psychic states of the reader belong to the structure of the literary work. Author and work are heterogeneous, reader and work equally so. Psychologism is rejected. We need to focus on the work itself with no regard to the author's psychology or that of the reader. Ingarden thus would sympathize with what William K. Wimsatt has called the "intentional fallacy." Intentions do not matter: only the work. All this has been argued, with some amplifications and examples, in my *Theory of Literature* and is not, of course, absolutely new. T. S. Eliot, e.g., was convinced that "the difference between art and the event is absolute."[9]

Ingarden makes, I think, a major advance into the problems of literary theory when he analyzes the "structure of the literary work of art" by distinguishing four layers or strata in its makeup. These layers are conceived as conditioning each other: the second layer is impossible without the first, the third without the second, etc., and none can exist without the others. They are (1) the stratum of word-sounds which constitute (2) the meaning units. These present (3) schematized aspects and thus constitute (4) a world of represented objects. Moreover, Ingarden argues that great works of art present "metaphysical qualities" which may be absent in other works. Each stratum contributes to a whole, which, in optimal cases, achieves a "polyphonic harmony."

These strata need some elucidation. The sound stratum must not be confused with the actual articulation of sounds, e.g., in the declamation of a poem. Rather, Ingarden uses an idea similar to that of the phoneme in linguistics, though later he criticized Nikolay Trubetzkoy's conception and actually uses the term *word-sound* much more broadly.[10] The word-sound is unchangeable and intersubjective. Ingarden's sound stratum is not limited to what could be called sound in a strict sense. It includes rhythm, meter, sound-patterns, the physiognomy and the "feel" of words—features that might be classified as "connotations" and might be argued to belong rather to the second stratum, the units of meaning.

Be that as it may, Ingarden develops at great length a theory of the nature of meaning: first, the intentional directional factor of what we might call simple naming or reference; and second, the way in which a word can determine the qualitative properties of an object, its material features. A third manner of meaning Ingarden calls "forming" a "state of affairs," etc. Fictional objects would fall under this rubric. Ingarden discusses here the relationship between *langue* and *parole*, to use Ferdinand de Saussure's terms, the whole verbal context of a work, the

way a "state of affairs" is established. The peculiarity of Ingarden's discussion is its insistence on the view that the meaning units which constitute a purely intentional object thereby
lose contact with experience, lose "fullness" and concreteness, and become schematic: schemes that need to be interpreted, filled out, and in their purity remain necessarily ambiguous or, as he says, irridescent, opalescent. The meaning units
present a state of affairs or a world of objects which are "only
regarded as really existing without, figuratively speaking, being saturated with the character of reality." [11] Any declarative
sentence in a work of literature is a quasi-judgment. *Quasi-
judgment* seems to be a better term than I. A. Richards' similar
pseudo-statement, which devalues the utterances in a work of
literature. Quasi-judgments in Ingarden simply indicate that
they are not assertive judgments claiming truth. As Sir Philip
Sidney said long ago, "the poet nothing affirmeth and therefore never lieth." Ingarden is consistent in arguing that propositional or factual statements in a work of art become assimilat-
ed to the fictional world and have to be interpreted as part and
parcel of that world. To give my own example: the description
of the printing house at the beginning of Balzac's *Lost Illusions*
has a different status from what it would have been in a pam-
phlet of the time, though the text may be identical and though
we hardly doubt the factual accuracy of the description. It
functions within the novel and the accuracy of the account does
not matter. In a historical novel one may read, "It was extremely cold on January 20, 1624." In a novel this statement
does not require verification from weather reports. In a history
book it may. Similarly, propositional statements such as the
first sentence of Tolstoy's *Anna Karenina* ("Happy families are
all alike; every unhappy family is unhappy in its own way")
need not be debated as to their validity, but have their function
in the subsequent development of the novel. We have to take
Browning, or rather Pippa, asserting that "God's in His heav-
en, all's right with the world," or Leopardi declaring, "Il
mondo è fango" (the world is mud), as dramatic statements

that cannot be discussed in isolation. Quasi-judgments are not, Ingarden argues, either genuine judgments or mere assumptions (*Annahmen*, a term from Meinong).[12] They merely constitute the state of affairs, the objects to which they lend the semblance or illusion of reality. For Ingarden the quasi-judgment is the feature that constitutes the "literariness" of a work of art. But this seems a vicious circle: we recognize a work of art by its making quasi-judgments, but how do we know that they are quasi-judgments? In *The Literary Work of Art*, Ingarden is content to say that we recognize a novel, a play, or a poem by its title or subtitle, by some announcement of its genre. But later, in *On the Cognition of a Literary Work of Art*, he tries to define the specifics of literary language in the terms made familiar by the Russian formalists: a specific vocabulary, the rhythm, the intonation, the metaphorical style, the ambiguity of phrasing. This may be true of much poetry and poetic prose but it is, I think, insufficient to set off the novel or rather most novels using everyday language from a nonfictional work.

The meaning units intend a represented world. This world is in relation to the actual world but differs from it profoundly, e.g., in the way time and space function in it. Ingarden analyzes carefully the differences between empirical time and time in fiction, represented time. Real time, e.g., is continuous, while represented time appears in isolated segments; in real time we cannot retrieve the past, while in represented time a past moment can be as vivid as a present one.

A logical consequence of this view is that the fictional world contains "spots of indeterminacy," blank, empty spots. Every real object is fully determined, and in experiencing it we can always discover new determinations. In contrast a fictional object will have a limited number of qualities which seem to demand a filling out or what Ingarden calls a "concretization." It is not always quite clear whether we should do so or whether we may refrain from doing so. Filling out seems to be largely matching with the real world: e.g., we may not be told whether a character in a novel is tall or short, blond or dark, and we are free to supply these determinants in imagination. The filling out, for instance, by an illustrator or a moviemaker or a producer of a play who has "concretized" his object wrongly (so we may think) may annoy and upset us as it violates our own "concretization."

Narrowing down these choices is then the function of the third stratum, that of "schematized aspects." To give Ingarden's example from a novel by Romain Rolland, *L'Âme enchantée*, the various Paris streets mentioned are presented by their sights and sounds.[13] Only a person who has been to Paris can imagine them in their concrete actuality: a person who has never been to Paris will have to fill these empty spots by drawing on his possibly very different experiences of streets in other cities. An event in a novel may be presented as seen or heard: even the same event, e.g., the banging of a door, as Claudia Chauchat bangs it in Thomas Mann's *The Magic Mountain*. Or a character may be presented purely by his external characteristics such as the tics common in comedy or the novels of Dickens, or he may be presented only or almost exclusively by the inner events of his mind. Raskolnikov, for example, is hardly described; he may seem a disembodied soul of whose motivations and inner struggles we know much more than of his exterior. Ingarden includes figurative language or the proper use of the sound stratum with the factors that hold schematic aspects in readiness.

I find it difficult to isolate this stratum of schematic aspects from that of represented objects, but Ingarden draws a distinction between "intuitive appearances" and conceptual meanings which alone constitute intentional objects. The world of the work must not be confused with the real world. Dickens' London is not the real London, nor is Kafka's Prague the Prague of the early twentieth century, just as Edgar Allan Poe's horrendous castles are not in Germany or Virginia.

Ingarden then at the end of his descriptive analysis suggests that some, and these would be great, works of art present an "Idea" or at least "metaphysical qualities." They do not constitute an indispensable stratum: they emerge only in some great works. Ingarden gives examples of what he calls, I think somewhat misleadingly, "metaphysical qualities" which seem to include almost any work of literature except the most trivial: "the sublime, the tragic, the dreadful, the moving, the inexplicable, the demonic, the holy, the sinful, the sorrowful, the indescribable serenity of happiness, as well as the grotesque, the charming, the light, the peaceful." [14] These qualities are not properties of objects, or traits or psychic states, but manifest themselves in situations and events. Ingarden becomes rapturous when he describes the "ecstasy" with which we may see these manifestations that come to us as a "grace" and make life worth living. [15]

More soberly, Ingarden broaches the problem of "truth" in literature and the "idea" embodied in a work of art. He is careful to avoid the intellectualistic misunderstanding of art. Literature cannot be "true" in the literal sense. Truth in literature means rather objective consistency, some analogue to the nature of reality. The "idea" of a work of art is thus not a propositional truth but is contained in "an essential connection . . . between a specific life-situation . . . and a metaphysical quality." [16] I am not sure I understand this fully: *Idea* seems to be here a variant of the term *symbol*.

Throughout *The Literary Work of Art* Ingarden insisted that the work is not a temporal sequence. It exists simultaneously in all its parts and "none of these parts is earlier or later in a temporal sense." But in chapter eleven of the second section, Ingarden recognizes that it also presents a sequential order. If we would reverse the order of sentences in a work, the meaning would become scrambled and even become nonsense.

In a last section, called "Supplements and Consequences," Ingarden sketches what became the main theme of his second book, *On the Cognition of a Literary Work of Art*: the idea of the "concretization" of the work and hence of its "life" in history. "Concretization" is not, as we might think, the result of the individual reader's acts of apprehension. They are individual concretizations, not simply "subjective" responses. "Only a theorizing literary critic," he says, "could hit upon the bizarre idea of looking for the literary work in the soul of the reader." Concretizations have their base in subjective acts but are also rooted in the literary work itself. Ingarden insists on the distinction between the literary work and its concretizations. It seems hard to see how they can be distinguished in practice, if, as Ingarden admits, we can know the work only in its concretizations. But, he answers, "a concretization is not a cloak that impedes access to the work of art itself. The individual differences among concretizations enable us to establish what belongs to the work itself and what belongs to the concretizations conditioned by contingencies." [17] Apparently the student can isolate the literary work itself by comparing many experiences of the work and identifying the work itself as that part of the multiple experiences which remains constant. The differences between the work as such and the concretization will appear in the different strata; thus in the sound-stratum a good recital may add to the value or effect of the virtual, prescribed sounds. Ingarden recognizes, however, that a concretization can deviate significantly from the work and thus may become simply a new work, more or less related to the original. The problem of falsifying concretizations is regulated by literary criticism which has the task of reconstructing a work in its context, to see to it that it is interpreted correctly. Ingarden thus adopts a version of the logician Gottlob Frege's distinction between *Sinn* (sense) and *Bedeutung* (meaning), "sense" being constant, "meaning" changing in time with the different interpretations.

If meaning changes, it changes in history. One can argue that a work of art has a "life" in history, in two figurative senses. It lives "while it is expressed in a manifold of concretizations" and it lives while it undergoes changes as a result of ever new concretizations. One can imagine a history of concretizations, say, of Shakespeare's *Hamlet* which would use evidence from criticisms, theatrical performances, Hamlet figures in fiction and drama, etc. Thus history of criticism, history of the afterlife of a work, in a wide sense would acquire great importance. But how far, one may ask, can one speak of the work of art having undergone change? Ingarden answers that a work may have changed, e.g., through the changes in language (say Chaucer) but still retains some "structure of determinancy." [18]

Only in the very last chapter does Ingarden face the problem of value. He sees it in the "polyphonic harmony" of the four strata.[19] But this harmony is apparently not realized unless it is expressed in a concretization. The last sentences of the book express some surprise and even puzzlement:

> The literary work is a true miracle. It exists and lives and effects us, it enriches our life extraordinarily, it gives us hours of rapture and allows us to descend into the very depths of existence, and yet it is only a heteronomous construct which in the sense of an autonomy of being is Nothing . . . a "Nothing" and yet a wonderful world apart even though it comes into being and exists only by our grace.[20]

Nothing is said, however, about the nature of values. I was, I still believe, entirely correct in criticizing Ingarden for ignoring the problem of criticism as evaluation in this book. At the time of my writing *Theory of Literature*, I did not and could not know the later book *On the Cognition of a Literary Work of Art*, nor his later attempts to come to terms with the problem of value. Ingarden himself says that he analyzed the structure of the work of art in such a way that it includes both valuable and valueless work. He postponed the problem of value to his later writings: a decision I had not clearly realized.

On the Cognition of the Literary Work of Art repeats much of the argumentation of the earlier book from a new perspective. The same problems are now seen from the point of view of the reader. Some new ideas are introduced. The earlier book thought of the strata as an almost static pyramid of layers, rising one above the other vertically. The new book sees that we experience a work of art in a temporal order, in a process of reading which Ingarden analyzes with great subtlety. He elaborately distinguishes between different kinds of reading: passive, mere enjoyment, for amusement; and active reading, which assumes two forms—reading which has as its aim an investigative, intellectual grasp of the work, or, finally, reading which submits to the aesthetic qualities. Much ingenuity is spent in differentiating between these different kinds of reading, although, I think, it would be difficult in practice to keep them apart, to prevent their mixing and our shifting between them.

Ingarden is mostly concerned with the way we constitute the different strata in reading. He shows, for instance, that we build the fourth stratum, the world of represented objects, in a different order from the order in which we read the sentences bearing units of meaning. For example, we build the image of a person from scattered remarks of a person himself or from references to him in order to construe a living character, or we put together events which may, as for example in Faulkner's *Absalom, Absalom!* or Ibsen's *Rosmersholm*, be revealed in a sequence not identical with the sequence of the parts of the novel or play. At the end of a reading we try to synthesize all the strata of a work of art in a unity which Ingarden insists can only metaphorically be called an "organism." [21] It is only analogous to an organism in the integration of parts in the whole, in the necessity of a hierarchy of parts, in the dominance of a main function. Ingarden rejects what is commonly called the main function of a work of art: the expression of the personality of the author, though he recognizes that works of art have served as confessions of an author and may even be almost indistinguishable from diaries or letters, or may at least be continuous with them. There are love poems, he admits, which are indubitably addressed to a specific person for a specific purpose, e.g., to persuade a woman to return the poet's love, but the moment these poems are printed and are contemplated as works of art and not as a source of information about the life of the author, they cease to be expressions of a personality. Similarly, looking for the idea, or ideology, or the practical purpose of a work of art deprives it of its aesthetic value. But Ingarden insists that this view is not "idea-free aestheticism." [22] It merely asserts that a work of art has aesthetic value and would cease to be a work of art if it were reduced to other values. But he rejects formalism in the sense of the Russian formalists: the work is not a sum of its devices. [23] It is not merely language: rather it projects a world of represented objects.

Ingarden then broaches the problem largely ignored in the earlier book, the fact that we read every work in time, that it is apprehended as a time structure. Ingarden uses the Bergsonian idea of *durée*, of an immediate present which is not a single point of time, but has "duration," extension, and he worries about the perspective foreshortening as it inevitably happens in the course of reading. We are never able to keep the totality of a work in active memory. Reading is not only a process of foreshortening, but it requires also anticipation: we sense the coming events, we anticipate, for instance, the rhymes in a stanza. Much is made of the perspective in time and its differences from perspective in space. He distinguishes different "distances" in time, denying what Proust asserted, that there is the possibility of a genuine return to the past. [24] Ingarden describes the process of what he calls "receding into the past" while reading, the way we often change or even falsify events in the light of other happenings.

This leads him to other ideas absent in the earlier book. He argues for the differences of genres in a novel way. At first the distinction seems old enough: the present tense prevails in drama and some lyrical poems; the simple past localizes a text in historical time. But by introducing the concept of temporal distance he makes persuasive distinctions. He quotes lyrical poems that are outside time, extratemporal, such as Goethe's "Über allen Gipfeln" or the final piece in Rilke's *Book of Images*, beginning "Death is great." [25] Ingarden describes experiencing such poems as a living into the moment of the poem, as an experience of identification, as an abolition of the difference between subject and object, something like the *epoché* of Husserl. But in the drama, though it also occurs in the present, an inevitable time distance is created by the very presence of the spectator.[26]

New, also, is the emphasis on the distinction between the work of art and the aesthetic object, between artistic and aesthetic values. The Venus de Milo is merely a piece of marble. We have to forget its physical features when we constitute it as an aesthetic object. We would be revolted by a woman without arms or feel sorry for her if we saw the piece of marble only as a simulacrum of a woman; but the lack of arms does not disturb us if we contemplate it as an aesthetic object.[27] The experiencing of an aesthetic object, however, Ingarden argues, is not one of pleasure. The aesthetic experience requires rather an isolation of the object, a concentration of attention on it, a focusing on its pure quality. The aesthetic experience is not purely passive contemplation but an active perceiving of quality. Ingarden does not like the theory of empathy as propounded by Theodor Lipps and his followers because it is psychological, but frankly I find it difficult to distinguish between his phenomenological, generalizing analyses and descriptive psychology.

Ultimately the process of reading leads to the establishment of a quality of harmony, which is usually called *Gestalt* or structure, though Ingarden avoids the latter term and its association with the structuralist movement as it seems to him a term with too many different meanings. This constitution of a harmony is for Ingarden the last step in the formation of the aesthetic object. We respond to it, acknowledging its value or rejecting it as "ugly" or at least as "unsuccessful" as a work of art. We acknowledge the existence of a new work of art in an act which Ingarden calls an "as if"—a version of Coleridge's formula of the "willing suspension of disbelief."[28]

The work of art, we are told constantly, is a schematic structure: yet has an unchangeable skeleton. Ingarden thus makes a distinction between the work of art which is aesthetically neutral and has artistic value, and the aesthetic object which has aesthetic value. Artistic value is purely relational: it prepares the means for the constitution of the aesthetic object which is present only in its concretizations. Ingarden has to admit that some readers find this distinction obscure. They argue that there are only concretizations. But Ingarden objects to what to him would lead to relativism. We can, he argues, compare concretizations, and also we can refrain from filling the spots of indeterminancy. He gives an example from Mann's story "Tristan." The death of Mrs. Klöterjahn is implied by the pulling of the curtains. It is not a spot of indeterminancy. It is a fact, though inferred and not directly stated, even though the details of her death remain undetermined. We can refrain from imagining them and probably should refrain. The example is used to prove that we can point to spots of indeterminancy and still grasp a work in its schematic structure.[29] The artistic value is in the potentialities for filling the empty spots. Thus pre-aesthetic analysis anticipates the different possibilities of concretization. Formal analysis is possible: Ingarden does not disdain even statistics as long as we realize that they are only to be used as a means of recognizing traits or confirming observations. He gives as an example the beginning of Mann's *Buddenbrooks*, which shows a company in a drawing room and consists largely of description. Nouns and adjectives with visual connotations prevail statistically.[30] In examining a Rilke poem we can observe the rhymes and their functioning. All this shows that we can study a work as distinct from its concretizations.[31] We can say that the work prepares and determines the concretization. We can control these effects by studying the poet's drafts or we can make our own substitutions to see how changes in words or in the order of events would affect the aesthetic object.[32]

Ingarden thus prescribes new tasks for literary scholarship: to ascertain the empty spots, to find out which empty spots we are allowed to remove and which should remain empty. We should ask what the limits of variability in an empty spot are, and finally what aesthetic qualities are constituted by filling these empty spots. Works and genres will differ: e.g., in some lyrics the silence, the undetermined, the unsaid should remain undisturbed. Scholars who reduce a poet to a philosopher are condemned.[33]

Ingarden reflects on varying incidence of concretizations and their effects. Great works of art, the *Iliad*, the Greek tragedies, the plays of Shakespeare, the poems of Goethe, go through concretizations in every age. The share of the works themselves diminishes. Responsibility for the actualization of aesthetic value passes more and more to the reader. Great works have, paradoxically, only a relatively small share in the constitution of aesthetic values, though Ingarden recognizes that there are other types of works, self-enclosed, dense works, which resist a great variation of concretizations.[34] Thus Ingarden denies that there are general criteria of valuation, though he asserts and reasserts the view that values are not relative or subjective; he only deplores the lack of an adequate language to describe aesthetic values. He welcomes Wittgenstein's return to an analysis of ordinary language as it may increase our awareness of shades of meaning. In a special paper he made an attempt to classify aesthetic values; unfortunately I do not here have the space to expound his complicated system.

The investigative cognition of a work of art is kept distinct from the aesthetic experience of it which is achievable only in a concretization. Inevitably Ingarden raises the question of the adequacy and legitimacy of certain concretizations. He condemns, for example, modern stage managers who ruthlessly transform a work in order to achieve a stage effect.[36] In Ingarden's view the response to values should be sharply distinguished from the values themselves. He complains that wrong conclusions are drawn from the fact that, say, the plays of Shakespeare were not appreciated in a certain time. One may argue that the work has no value in itself, that there are simply changing value responses or impositions which we merely project at the object itself. Ingarden answers that one may be blind to values which, nonetheless exist independently of value responses. Values are founded in the object and need not be appreciated or judged in order to exist.[37] In interpreting a work of art we have to be able to make comparisons and judgments as to the value of different concretizations. Ingarden introduces the concept of "proximity" to the original work or the concept of "doing justice" to it, though he recognizes that there cannot be an absolute "proximity." He prefers the performance of Molière by the Comédie française or a play by the Stanislavsky group that transmits the conventions of the original performances, to modern adaptations.[38] Ingarden dislikes or professes not to understand the term *norm* but here and in his constant preference for "harmonious unity"[39] one sees that he himself upholds traditional norms of "classical," well-organized art. He sees that we live in an age in which this unity and harmony are not highly valued. He considers this a sign of decadence, of the loss of center, alluding to Hans Sedlmayr's book, *Der Verlust der Mitte*, which must be considered as an extreme condemnation of all modernist art.[40] Ingarden pleads, at the end, for a dialogue among students and scholars, for an agreement on basic problems and terms, for a "science of literature" which is not, of course, a natural science but still a body of knowledge which he feels would progress if the distinctions he has drawn should be understood and widely accepted. What is needed, he recognizes, is an aesthetic education which is open to everybody but for which not everybody is prepared nor everybody gifted enough to accomplish.[41] Still, objectivity in the sense of a consensus of experts, can be achieved in literary studies.

The book contains many new ideas and acute analyses but suffers to my mind from the repetitiousness and prolixity with which he belabors some of these problems. I am afraid that my own exposition, though much simplified, suggests both the richness of Ingarden's book and also its tortuous grappling with his insights.

Some of Ingarden's smaller writings are of great interest to the student of literature. There is a lecture dating from 1935 on the "Subject and Tasks of Literary Scholarship" which makes good distinctions between a general philosophical theory of literature, a "science of literature" which is either descriptive or historical, and literary criticism. The emphasis on a "characterology," a concept similar to Croce's *caracteristica*, of individual works appeals to me and I like his criticism of the supposed necessity of knowing all kinds of historical information for the understanding of a work of art. He cites the example of Dante's *Divine Comedy* which, we are told and often assume, was understood better by Dante's contemporaries who recognized the historical personages there represented or alluded to. Ingarden argues that they merely add facts to the stratum of represented objects which do not occur in the text. They did not understand the work better than we do, but worse; they falsified it by external information. It is a mistake to argue that we should reconstitute what Dante had in mind at the time of his writing, as neither the thought nor the experiences of an author matter, but only the results of his thoughts and experiences.[42] A similiar argument could be made for neglecting the identity of the authors satirized by Pope in the *Dunciad*.

Besides a "characterology" Ingarden recognizes a "typology" of literary works, considering these disciplines strictly descriptive, objective, nonevaluative. Evaluation is relegated to literary criticism which requires an aesthetic attitude. Ingarden, in accordance with his own preoccupations, stresses the ontology of a literary work of art, the philosophical or rather phenomenological analysis of its mode of being and structure carried out in *The Literary Work of Art*.

A later piece on "Poetics" (1941–42) rehearses the same distinctions but now gives room to poetics, which Ingarden distinguishes from the purely descriptive "typology" of literature as a general theory of the essential structures, properties, and relations of a literary work of art. The difference between poetics and "typology" is, according to Ingarden's newly acquired conviction, that something like an *a priori* insight into the essence of genres is possible, that the enterprise of, say, defining the nature of the drama, the lyric, and the epic, is not in vain. We have seen that in *On the Cognition of a Literary Work of Art*, Ingarden uses the concept of "time-distance" to distinguish between the lyric, the novel, and the drama. Ingarden argues then against the attempt of formalists and linguists to absorb poetics into linguistics. A literary work of art is more than a linguistic construct. The world of represented objects cannot be absorbed into the underlying strata of sound and units of meaning.[43]

Ingarden's original scheme of the strata of a work of art seems to me a major contribution to literary theory. Also the way Ingarden defined the mode of existence of a literary work of art and thus determined its relation to psychology, biography, sociology, etc. seems to me convincing. His analysis of the strata, with its strong emphasis on the comparative independence of the represented objects, allows a rejection of the claims of what I call linguistic imperialism. His concept of concretization has given a new stimulus to an investigation of readers' reactions, to what has since come to be called *Rezeptionsaesthetik* (although its proponents derive rather from Heidegger and Gadamer). The concept of "spots of indeterminancy" has proved particularly fruitful and has been developed, e.g., in Wolfgang Iser's *The Implied Reader*.[44]

Still, I have some reservations. The distinction between "sense" and "meaning" taken up in E. D. Hirsch's *Validity in Interpretation*[45] or the similar distinction between artistic and aesthetic values are difficult or impossible to maintain in literary criticism, though I welcome Ingarden's defense of a structure of determinancy of a work of art which persists throughout the history of concretizations and allows us to postulate the ideal of correct interpretation. I have my doubts whether one can keep the schematized aspects apart from the represented objects and there are, of course, many questions of literary theory Ingarden hardly touches on. Ingarden remains a philosopher and aesthetician, which is nothing to complain about, though it does reduce his usefulness and appeal to a student of concrete literature.

Notes

BENEDETTO CROCE

1. *Goethe*, trans. Emily Anderson, Intro. by Douglas Ainslie (New York: Alfred A. Knopf, 1923); *The Poetry of Dante*, trans. Douglas Ainslie (New York: Henry Holt, 1922); *Ariosto, Shakespeare, Corneille*, trans. Douglas Ainslie (New York: Henry Holt, 1920); *European Literature in the Nineteenth Century*, trans. Douglas Ainslie (London: Chapman and Hall, 1924; reprint ed., New York: Haskell House, 1969); *Philosophy, Poetry, History*, trans. Cecil Sprigge (London: Oxford University Press, 1966) The best book in English is Gian N. G. Orsini, *Benedetto Croce: Philosopher of Art and Literary Critic* (Carbondale, Ill.: Southern Illinois University Press, 1961).

2. "Breviario di Estetica," in *Nuovi Saggi di Estetica* (3rd ed.; Bari: Laterza, 1948), p. 62; *Guide to Aesthetics*, trans. Patrick Romanell (Indianapolis: Regnery-Gateway, 1965), pp. 55–56.

3. *Estetica* (8th ed.; Bari: Laterza, 1946), p. 41; *Aesthetic*, trans. Douglas Ainslie (2nd ed.; London: Macmillan, 1922), p. 36.

4. *Nuovi Saggi*, pp. 15–16; *Guide*, p. 14.

5. *Estetica*, p. 19; *Aesthetic*, p. 16. *Nuovi Saggi*, p. 34; *Guide*, p. 31.

6. *Estetica*, p. 81; *Aesthetic*, p. 72.

7. *Estetica*, p. 128; *Aesthetic*, p. 117. *Nuovi Saggi*, p. 38; *Guide*, p. 36. *Estetica*, p. 126; *Aesthetic*, p. 114.

8. *Estetica*, pp. 44, 42–43; *Aesthetic*, pp. 38, 37. *Nuovi Saggi*, p. 48; *Guide*, p. 44.

9. *Nuovi Saggi*, p. 35; *Guide*, p. 33.

10. *Estetica*, p. 57; *Aesthetic*, p. 51.

11. *La Poesia* (4th ed.; Bari: Laterza, 1946), pp. 9, 10.

12. *La Poesia di Dante* (6th ed.; Bari: Laterza, 1948), p. 24; *The Poetry of Dante*, p. 35.

13. *Problemi di estetica* (4th ed.; Bari: Laterza, 1949), p. 155.

14. *Nuovi Saggi*, p. 222.

15. *Problemi di estetica*, p. 73.

16. *Nuovi Saggi*, pp. 157–97.

17. *Storia della età barocca in Italia* (2nd ed.; Bari: Laterza, 1946), p. 235.

18. *Goethe* (4th ed.; Bari: Laterza, 1946), pp. 16, 52; *Goethe* (English trans.), pp. 27–28, 82.

19. *Poesia e non poesia* (4th ed.; Bari: Laterza, 1946), p. 61; *European Literature in the Nineteenth Century*, p. 68.

20. *La filosofia di Giambattista Vico* (Bari: Laterza, 1910); *The Philosophy of Giambattista Vico*, trans. R. G. Collingwood (London: Oxford University Press, 1913).

PAUL VALÉRY

1. The best book available in English is Jean Hytier, *La Poétique de Valéry* (Paris: Armand Colin, 1953), translated as *The Poetics of Paul Valéry* by Richard Howard (Garden City, N.Y.: Doubleday, 1966). There is a fine paper by Ralph Freedman, "Valéry: Protean Critic," in *Modern French Criticism*, ed. John K. Simon (Chicago: University of Chicago Press, 1972), pp. 1–40.

2. A facsimile edition of the *Cahiers* covering the years 1894–1945 has appeared in 1957–61 in 29 volumes. It fills 26,600 pages. Two volumes of a printed transcript, edited by Judith Robinson, were published in 1973–74 in the Pléiade series (Paris: Gallimard).

3. *Oeuvres*, ed. Jean Hytier (2 vols.; Paris: Bibliothèque de la Pléiade, 1957–60), 2:801, 1:1346; *The Collected Works of Paul Valéry*, ed. Jackson Mathews (15 vols.; Princeton, N.J.: Princeton University Press, 1956–75), 14:391, 13:96.

4. "Réflexions sur l'art," a lecture printed in *Bulletin de la Société française de Philosophie*, 35 (1935): 64, found in *Collected Works* 13:143; not given in *Oeuvres*, but see vol. 1, p. 1817.

5. "Réflexions," p. 63; *Collected Works* 13:142.

6. "Réflexions," p. 64; *Collected Works* 13:143.

7. *Oeuvres* 1:1348; *Collected Works* 13:98.

8. *Oeuvres* 1:534, 538; *Collected Works* 6:151, 156–57.

9. *Oeuvres* 1:154–67; *Collected Works* 8:161–76.

10. *Oeuvres* 2:1516, 1:1415; *Collected Works* 15:302, 13:69.

11. *Oeuvres* 1:1349; *Collected Works* 13:100.

12. Frédéric Lefèvre, *Entretiens avec Paul Valéry* (Paris: Le Livre, 1926), p. 109.

13. *Oeuvres* 1:1415, 1321, 1204–5, 1490; *Collected Works* 13:69, 7:60, 8:71, 7:131.

14. *Oeuvres* 1:1363, 476; *Collected Works* 7:198, 11.

15. *Oeuvres* 1:1464–90; *Collected Works* 7:100–32.

16. *Oeuvres* 2:1530, 546, 1515, 1:1335, 1335–36, 2:667; *Collected Works* 15:324, 14:96, 15:301, 7:76, 77, 14:235.

17. *Oeuvres* 1:453, 2:801, 635; *Collected Works* 7:289, 14:390–91, 209.

18. *Oeuvres* 2:642, 764; *Collected Works* 14:218, 347.

19. *Oeuvres* 2:866, 1:555; *Collected Works* 14:470, 9:177.

20. *Oeuvres* 2:1533; *Collected Works* 15:328.

21. *Oeuvres* 2:866, 1:572, 565, 1471–72; *Collected Works* 14:469, 9:199, 190, 7:109.

22. Valéry uses the term in *Cahiers* in 1911 (4:488). He claims to have "started the expression going" (*Cahiers* 11:877, 1926 or early 1927). The term "pure poetry" is, however, quite frequent in English, in Joseph Warton, Leigh Hunt, etc.

23. *Oeuvres* 1:1275–76, 1276, 1451; *Collected Works* 7:46, 46–47, 185.

24. Lefèvre, *Entretiens*, pp. 65–66.

25. *Oeuvres* 1:1453, 1457; *Collected Works* 7:180, 185.

26. *Oeuvres* 2:638, 1:1509, 2:638–39; *Collected Works* 14:213, 7:156, 14:213.

27. *Oeuvres* 1:1501–3; *Collected Works* 7:146–47.

28. *Oeuvres* 1:1324 (cf. 1:784); *Collected Works* 7:63 (cf. 8:324).

29. *Oeuvres* 1:1456, 2:113, 483, 1:1423, 2:640, 1460; *Collected Works* 7:183, 4:108, 14:17, 11:88, 14:216, 7:189.

30. *Oeuvres* 1:584, 710, 657, 589, 2:1515; *Collected Works* 7:253, 8:298, 289, 7:258, 15:301.

31. *Oeuvres* 1:1245, 2:679, 635, 1:485; *Collected Works* 8:124, 238, 14:209, 7:22.

32. *Bulletin de la Société française de Philosophie* 31 (1931): 118, found in *Collected Works* 13:142; not given in *Oeuvres*.

33. *Oeuvres* 1:1476, 1333, 1505, 651, 649; *Collected Works* 7: 114, 74, 150, 8:281, 279.

34. *Oeuvres* 1:651; *Collected Works* 8:282.

35. *Oeuvres* 1:1440; *Collected Works* 13:86.

36. *Oeuvres* 1:480, 1137, 1254, 590, 1279; *Collected Works* 7:16, 10:128, 7:160, 14:150, 7:51.

37. Quoted in Charles Du Bos, *Journal 1921–23* (Paris: Corrêa, 1946), p. 222.

38. *Oeuvres* 2:714, 1:374–75, 2:893, 773; *Collected Works* 14: 282–83, 562:63, 505, 359.

39. *Oeuvres* 1:508; *Collected Works* 11:195.

40. *Oeuvres* 1:1814 quotes letter to Jean Prévost, May 16, 1943, first published in *Confluences*, no. 21–24, July–August 1943; not in *Collected Works*.

41. *Oeuvres* 2:1530, 1506, 1530; *Collected Works* 15:324, 288, 324.

42. *Oeuvres* 1:770, 771, 2:1515, 1:771–72, 2:638; *Collected Works* 9:296, 297, 15:302, 9:297–98, 14:213.

43. "Amphion" and "Sémiramis," in *Oeuvres* 2:166–96; *Collected Works* 3:223–309.

44. *Oeuvres* 2:1524; *Collected Works* 15:314–15.

45. Preface to Lucien Fabre, *Dieu est innocent* (Paris: Nagel, 1946), pp. xiv–xv, in *Collected Works* 7:239; not in *Oeuvres*.

46. Preface to Fabre, *Dieu est innocent*, p. xv, in *Collected Works* 7:239–40.

47. *Oeuvres* 2:1329, 1:796; *Collected Works* 12:109, 9:18.

48. *Oeuvres* 1:1509; *Collected Works* 7:155–56.

49. *Oeuvres* 1:1496–1506, 1507–14; *Collected Works* 7:140–52, 153–58.

50. *Oeuvres* 1:1509, 1507, 2:678, 557; *Collected Works* 7:155, 152, 14:236, 109.

51. "Un éloge de la virtuosité," *Centenaire de Paganini* (Nice, 1940), reprinted in *Vues* (Paris: Le Choix, La Table Ronde, 1948), p. 357; not given in *Collected Works* or *Oeuvres*.

52. *Oeuvres* 1:494, 2:478; *Collected Works* 7:33, 14:10.

53. "Réflexions sur l'art" p. 64; in *Collected Works* 13:144; not given in *Oeuvres*.

54. *Oeuvres* 1:373–74, 817; *Collected Works* 14:562, 9:44.

55. *Oeuvres* 1:817; *Collected Works* 9:44.

GEORG LUKÁCS

1. *Georg Lukács und der Revisionismus* (Berlin: Aufbau-Verlag, 1960).

The chapter on "Lukács as a Theoretician of Literature" in Peter Demetz, *Marx, Engels, and the Poets*, trans. Jeffrey L. Sammons (Chicago: University of Chicago Press, 1967), is still the best treatment in English. There are good essays in G. H. R. Parkinson's *Georg Lukács: The Man, His Work, and His Ideas* (London: Weidenfels and Nicolson, 1970). *Georg Lukács* by Ehrhard Bahr and Ruth Goldschmidt Kunzer (New York: Frederick Ungar, 1972) is a well-informed general monograph. George Lichtheim, *Lukács* (London: Fontana Modern Masters, 1970), is disappointing. The chapter "The Case for Georg Lukács" in Fredric Jameson, *Marxism and Form* (Princeton, N.J.: Princeton University Press, 1971), is strictly Marxist in outlook as is the descriptive book *György Lukács* by Bela Királyfalvi (Princeton, N.J.: Princeton University Press, 1975). Victor Zitta, *Georg Lukács' Marxism: Alienation, Dialectics, Revolution; a Study in Utopia and Ideology* (The Hague: Martinus Nijhoff, 1961), is harshly critical of Lukács as a person and thinker.

2. *Probleme des Realismus* 1:354, from "Es geht um den Realismus." I translate from the German editions of Lukács's work, mostly collected in *Werke* (Neuwied: Luchterhand), consisting of *Probleme des Realismus* (3 vols.; 1971, 1964, 1965), *Deutsche Literatur in zwei Jahrhunderten* (1964), and *Aesthetik* (2 vols.; 1963).

3. *Die Seele und die Formen* (Neuwied: Luchterhand, 1971), p. 223; *Soul and Form* (London: Merlin Press, 1974), p. 155.

4. "Zwischen Klassik und Bolschewismus," *Merkur* 12 (1958): 514.

5. *Probleme der Aesthetik* (Neuwied: Luchterhand, 1969) contains almost all writings on the history of aesthetics.

6. English translations of relevant texts: *The Historical Novel*, trans. Hannah and Stanley Mitchell (London: Merlin Press, 1962); *Studies in European Realism*, Intro. by Alfred Kazin (New York:

Grosset and Dunlap, 1964); *Realism in Our Time*, trans. John and Necke Mander, Intro. by George Steiner (New York: Harper and Row, 1964); *Essays on Thomas Mann*, trans. Stanley Mitchell (London: Merlin Press, 1964); *Goethe and His Age*, trans. Robert Anchor (New York: Grosset and Dunlap, 1969); *Solzhenitsyn*, trans. William David Graf (Cambridge, Mass.: MIT Press, 1969); *Writer and Critic*, trans. Arthur D. Kahn (London: Merlin Press, 1970); *The Theory of the Novel*, trans. Anna Bostock (Cambridge, Mass.: MIT Press, 1971); *Soul and Form*, trans. Anna Bostock (London: Merlin Press, 1974).

    7. *Aesthetik* 1:22, 229.

    8. Text of letter in Karl Marx–Friedrich Engels, *Über Kunst und Literatur: eine Sammlung aus ihren Schriften*, ed. Michail Lipschitz (Berlin [East]: 1948), pp. 103–4. On anticipations see my *History of Modern Criticism* (4 vols.; New Haven, Conn.: Yale University Press, 1955–65), *passim*, and see indexes under "Intention."

    9. *Studies in Classic American Literature* (Garden City, N.Y.: Doubleday, 1953), p. 13.

    10. *Probleme des Realismus* 1:13–22, "Willy Bredels Romane," and 1:35–54, "Reportage oder Gestaltung."

    11. Quoted in *Schriften zur Literatursoziologie*, ed. Peter Ludz (Neuwied: Luchterhand, 1961), p. 73, from Preface to the Hungarian *Evolutionary History of Modern Drama* (2 vols.; 1912), since translated into German as *Entwicklungsgeschichte des modernen Dramas* (Neuwied: Luchterhand, 1981), p. 12.

    12. *Aesthetik* 1:250.

    13. *Probleme des Realismus* 1:588, from "Die Gegenwartsbedeutung des kritischen Realismus"; cf. *Realism in Our Time*, p. 122.

    14. *Aesthetik* 1:270.

    15. *Solschenitzyn* (Neuwied: Luchterhand, 1969), p. 74; *Solzhenitsyn* (English trans.), p. 77.

    16. *Probleme des Realismus* 1:152, 156, from "Die intellektuelle Physiognomie des künstlerischen Gestaltens"; cf. *Writer and Critic*, pp. 151, 154.

    17. *Probleme des Realismus* 1:228, from "Erzählen oder Beschreiben?"; cf. *Writer and Critic*, p. 142.

    18. *Probleme des Realismus* 2:250, from "Tolstoi und die Probleme des Realismus"; cf. *Studies in European Realism*, p. 194.

    19. *Probleme des Realismus* 2:83, from "Gogol: Rede zu seinem hundersten Todestag."

20. *Probleme des Realismus* 2:331, from "Es geht um den Realismus."

21. *Lezioni sulla Divina Commedia*, ed. M. Manfredi (Bari: Laterza, 1955), p. 350.

22. *Probleme des Realismus* 1:501, from "Die Gegenwartsbedeutung des kritischen Realismus"; cf. *Realism in Our Time*, p. 48.

23. *Aesthetik* 1:296.

24. *Probleme des Realismus* 1:162, from "Die intellektuelle Physiognomie des künstlerischen Gestaltens"; cf. *Writer and Critic*, p. 161.

25. *Probleme des Realismus* 1:631, from "Kunst und objektive Wahrheit"; cf. *Writer and Critic*, pp. 49–50.

26. *Aesthetik* 1:763–66.

27. *Probleme des Realismus* 1:506, from "Die Gegenwartsbedeutung des kritischen Realismus"; cf. *Realism in Our Time*, p. 52.

28. *Skizze einer Geschichte der neueren deutschen Literatur* (Neuwied: Luchterhand, 1963), p. 87.

29. *Probleme des Realismus* 2:198, from "Tolstoi und die Probleme des Realismus"; cf. *Studies in European Realism*, p. 145.

30. *Probleme des Realismus* 2:161–76; cf. *Dostoevsky: A Collection of Critical Essays*, ed. Wellek (Englewood Cliffs, N.J.: Prentice-Hall, 1962), pp. 146–58.

31. *Hölderlin und die französische Revolution* (Neuwied: Luchterhand, 1969).

32. *Probleme des Realismus* 1:197–98; cf. *Writer and Critic*, pp. 110–11.

33. *Probleme des Realismus* 1:486 (see also 1:468), from "Die Gegenwartsbedeutung des kritischen Realismus"; cf. *Realism in Our Time*, p. 34 (see also pp. 17–18). See also *Aesthetik* 1:366.

34. *Probleme des Realismus* 1:467–68; cf. *Realism in Our Time*, pp. 17–18.

35. *Probleme des Realismus* 1:544–45; cf. *Realism in Our Time*, pp. 86–87.

36. *Probleme des Realismus* 1:534; cf. *Realism in Our Time*, p. 77.

37. *Probleme des Realismus* 1:496–97; cf. *Realism in Our Time*, pp. 43–44.

38. *Probleme des Realismus* 1:506, 535, 532; cf. *Realism in Our Time*, pp. 53, 78, 75.

39. *Probleme des Realismus* 1:109–49, "Grösse und Verfall des Expressionismus."

40. Ibid., p. 149.

41. Ibid., pp. 58–59, 63–64, from "Reportage oder Gestaltung."

42. *Schriften zur Literature und Kunst*, vol. 2 (Neuwied: Luchterhand, 1967), esp. pp. 105–8.

43. *Skizze einer Geschichte*, Preface, p. 6.

44. "Mitten im Aufstieg verliess er uns," in *Das neue Deutschland*, 21 August 1956.

45. *Probleme des Realismus* 1:261–62, from "Marx und das Problem des ideologischen Verfalls."

46. *Skizze einer Geschichte*, p. 172.

47. *Aesthetik* 1:267–68.

48. *Deutsche Literatur*, pp. 232–48, esp. p. 243.

49. Ibid., p. 76.

50. *Skizze einer Geschichte*, pp. 190–91.

51. See Thomas Mann, *Briefe, 1937–1947* (Wiesbaden: S. Fischer, 1963), p. 353, letter to C. B. Boutell, 21 January 1944. Mann refers there to Lukács's essay "Über Preussentum" in *Internationale Literatur*, no. 5 (1943), pp. 36–47, reprinted in *Thomas Mann* (5th ed.; Berlin: Aufbau-Verlag, 1957), pp. 174–75, which formulates the interpretation of "Death in Venice" much more cautiously. In a preface to the Hungarian edition of the stories of Thomas Mann (April 1955), reprinted in *Thomas Mann*, Lukács claims Mann's endorsement of his interpretation (p. 189). I am not aware of printed evidence unless Lukács refers to the general praise in *Die Entstehung des Doktor Faustus*; see *Gesammelte Werke* (Wiesbaden: S. Fischer, 1963), 11:240.

The best discussion is Dagmar Barnouw, "Flucht nach Utopia: Lukács und Thomas Mann," in Hans Rudolf Vaget and Dagmar Barnouw, *Thomas Mann: Studien zu seiner Rezeption* (Bern: Herbert Lang, 1975), pp. 109–28.

52. *Der historische Roman*, first published in Russian translation in 1938; the German original appeared first in East Berlin in 1955.

53. *Probleme des Realismus* 3:72; *The Historical Novel*, p. 60.

54. *Probleme des Realismus* 3:300–6; *The Historical Novel*, pp. 246–49.

55. *Probleme des Realismus* 1:578; *Realism in Our Time*, p. 115.

56. *Solschenitzyn*, p. 31; *Solzhenitsyn* (English trans.), p. 33.

57. *Aesthetik* 1:847.

58. Ibid., 2:675–872.

59. Ibid., p. 698.

60. Ibid., p. 126.

61. Ibid., 1:810.

62. Ibid., pp. 820, 842, 849.

ROMAN INGARDEN

1. *Das literarische Kunstwerk* (Halle: Niemeyer, 1931; 3rd ed., 1965).

2. "Über Seinsweise von Dichtung," in *Deutsche Vierteljahrschrift fur Literaturwissenschaft und Geistesgeschichte* 17 (1939): 137–52; reprinted in Günther Müller, *Morphologische Poetik* (Tübingen: Niemeyer, 1968), pp. 89–164.

3. *Vom Erkennen des literarischen Kunstwerks* (Tübingen: Niemeyer, 1968).

4. *Untersuchungen zur Ontologie der Kunst* (1962); *Erlebnis, Kunstwerk und Wert* (1969); and *Gegenstand und Aufgaben der Literaturwissenschaft*, ed. Rolf Fieguht (1976). All were published in Tübingen by Niemeyer.

5. *The Literary Work of Art*, trans. George G. Grabowicz, and *On the Cognition of a Literary Work of Art*, trans. Ann Crowley and Kenneth R. Olsen. Both were published in 1973 by Northwestern University Press, Evanston, Illinois.

6. "The Theory of Literary History," *Travaux du Cercle Linguistique de Prague* 6 (1936):173–91; *Literary Scholarship: Its Aims and Methods*, ed. Norman Foerster (Chapel Hill: University of North Carolina Press, 1941), pp. 91–103, 226–29, 239–55; "The Mode of Existence of a Literary Work," *Southern Review* 7 (1942):735–54, reprinted in *Critiques and Essays in Criticism, 1920–1948: Representing the Achievement of Modern British and American Critics*, ed. R. W. Stallman (New York: Wiley, 1949), pp. 210–23, and in Wellek, *Theory of Literature*.

Little has been written on Ingarden's literary theory in English. The seventy-page introduction by George Grabowicz to his translation of *The Literary Work of Art* is most instructive. There is also a good chapter in Robert R. Magliola, *Phenomenology and Literature* (West Lafayette, Ind.: Purdue University Press, 1977), pp. 107–41. A substantial monograph by Eugene H. Falk, *The Poetics of Roman*

Ingarden, has just (May 1981) been published by the University of North Carolina Press.

7. German translation: *Der Streit um die Existenz der Welt* (2 vols. in 3 parts; Tübingen: Niemeyer, 1964–65).

8. *Das literarische Kunstwerk*, p. 19; *Literary Work of Art*, p. 22.

9. T. S. Eliot, *Selected Essays* (London: Faber and Faber, 1932), p. 19.

10. *Gegenstand und Aufgaben*, pp. 117–24.

11. *Das literarische Kunstwerk*, p. 178; *Literary Work of Art*, p. 168.

12. *Das literarische Kunstwerk*, p. 176n; *Literary Work of Art*, p. 167n.

13. *Das literarische Kunstwerk*, p. 281; *Literary Work of Art*, p. 264.

14. *Das literarische Kunstwerk*, p. 310; *Literary Work of Art*, pp. 290–91.

15. *Das literarische Kunstwerk*, p. 312; *Literary Work of Art*, p. 292.

16. *Das literarische Kunstwerk*, p. 325; *Literary Work of Art*, p. 304.

17. *Das literarische Kunstwerk*, p. 359 and n; *Literary Work of Art*, pp. 336–37 and n.

18. *Das literarische Kunstwerk*, p. 394; *Literary Work of Art*, p. 368.

19. *Das literarische Kunstwerk*, p. 395; *Literary Work of Art*, p. 369.

20. *Das literarische Kunstwerk*, pp. 359–60; *Literary Work of Art*, p. 373.

21. *Vom Erkennen des literarischen Kunstwerks*, p. 74n; *On the Cognition of the Literary Work of Art*, p. 74n.

22. *Vom Erkennen*, p. 85; *Cognition*, p. 84.

23. *Vom Erkennen*, p. 85; *Cognition*, p. 85.

24. *Vom Erkennen*, p. 116; *Cognition*, p. 114.

25. *Vom Erkennen*, p. 140; *Cognition*, p. 136.

26. *Vom Erkennen*, p. 142; *Cognition*, p. 138.

27. *Vom Erkennen*, p. 191; *Cognition*, p. 184.

28. *Vom Erkennen*, p. 222; *Cognition*, p. 214.

29. *Vom Erkennen*, p. 253; *Cognition*, p. 244.

30. *Vom Erkennen*, p. 267; *Cognition*, p. 257.

31. *Vom Erkennen*, p. 282; *Cognition*, p. 272.

32. *Vom Erkennen*, p. 296; *Cognition*, p. 285.

33. *Vom Erkennen*, pp. 303–4; *Cognition*, pp. 292–93.

34. *Vom Erkennen*, pp. 309–10; *Cognition*, pp. 298–99.

35. *Vom Erkennen*, p. 332; *Cognition*, p. 319.

36. *Vom Erkennen*, p. 389n; *Cognition*, p. 373n.

37. *Vom Erkennen*, p. 397; *Cognition*, p. 381.

38. *Vom Erkennen*, p. 405n; *Cognition*, p. 388n.

39. *Vom Erkennen*, p. 421; *Cognition*, p. 403.

40. *Vom Erkennen*, p. 425n; *Cognition*, p. 407n.

41. *Vom Erkennen*, p. 437; *Cognition*, p. 418.

42. *Gegenstand und Aufgaben*, pp. 9–10.

43. Ibid., p. 56.

44. Wolfgang Iser, *The Implied Reader* (Baltimore, Md.: Johns Hopkins University Press, 1974); translation of *Der implizite Leser* (Munich: W. Fink, 1972).

45. E. D. Hirsch, Jr., *Validity in Interpretation* (New Haven, Conn.: Yale University Press, 1967).

Index